PENTALPHA

PENTALPHA

MICHELLE CERVANTES

NEW DEGREE PRESS

COPYRIGHT © 2020 MICHELLE CERVANTES

All rights reserved.

PENTALPHA

ISBN   978-1-64137-962-5   *Paperback*
       978-1-64137-787-4   *Kindle Ebook*
       978-1-64137-788-1   *Ebook*

To all the readers of paranormal fantasy who have been dying for a college-version story of magic, suspense, and love. You're welcome.

CONTENTS

PROLOGUE 11
CHAPTER 1 21
CHAPTER 2 55
CHAPTER 3 79
CHAPTER 4 129
CHAPTER 5 155
CHAPTER 6 191
CHAPTER 7 217
CHAPTER 8 233
CHAPTER 9 263
CHAPTER 10 289
ACKNOWLEDGMENTS 315

It is through darkness that we learn the most important lessons on this journey of life, but one must not forget the magic of the journey itself.

PROLOGUE

DEAR JOURNAL, SEPTEMBER 28TH, 2017, FRESHMAN YEAR

Sweat drips down my face. The sun's bright glare nearly blinds me as I carry the weight of my backpack on my shoulders, my hands gripping the suitcase so hard. The last thing I need is it to go rolling behind the sea of freshmen behind me. It feels like we've been walking up the hill for hours but we're barely a quarter of the way up. The parking lot feels like it's miles away while carrying all of this. Yet here's the good part: I still have more luggage in a large blue and yellow move-in cart housing provided us with. That cart holds my printer, fridge, bedding, and desk appliances that I could never carry up the hill. Luckily, UCLA has trucks filled with move-in carts to help us freshmen carry all of our things.

I never thought hauling my own luggage up a hill would be the hallmark of college dorming. But maybe it is. I remember this whole process from my summer program when I had two full carts filled with brand new dorm stuff from lamps to cute picturesque lights that ended up being thrown away. I've learned that I just need the basics with a slight twist: mandala-pattern bedding, a tie-dye-colored lamp, posters of my favorite car and actor, the necessities like school supplies plus technology, and a tapestry of my favorite painting from Alex Grey. It does have a uniqueness to it considering it looks straight out of a psychedelic festival, but I love it.

The foreground has two people embracing, portrayed in vibrant neon colors that show their inner layers from the muscular structure down to the bones, while the background has vibrant neon yellow and orange light rays. I love it so much because it reminds me of the weird aspects of myself. Being heavily immersed in the New Age movement will do that to you. I just wish the whole roommate situation wouldn't be random people.

My fear is getting a nightmare roommate like people vent about online. That or the fact that they might judge me for my love of the weirdness shown with my tapestry. They're probably going to think I am some weirdo hippy who loves tripping on psychedelics left and right or a flat-out stoner. I am neither of those things. I didn't make it to UCLA by doing anything impulsive like that. I originally chose the tapestry due to my love for anatomy and medicine.

I have always wanted to be a doctor ever since I was young. I wanted to help my community. Being low-income from a Mexican background, I have seen all the health disparities through my own and my parents' experience with the healthcare system. It needs to be improved immensely, and I will find a way to do that. Although I got a taste of the difficult chemistry class that I will have to take during my second year, I still think I can handle the rigor of the pre-med track. I will become someone of status, looking down upon those who doubted me because I am one of the very few Chicanas in medicine. I already can see it: Dr. Curanda Macias. It's only a matter of time before I fulfill that dream.

I finally make it to the crosswalk midway up the hill, where all the other freshmen gather in a crowd, waiting for the red hand to turn. The move-in truck with all the yellow and blue move-in carts passes in front of us, some freshmen having to move back onto the curve to avoid it. I hear more freshmen behind me, their breathing heavy while trying to talk.

"Are we at Hedrick yet?"

"We're only halfway up."

I start feeling the push of the line behind me as the stream of people gets closer. Finally, the light turns and the crowd in front starts to move. With every step I take, my heels begin to sting with more intensity. I take deep breaths to forget about it and continue following the flow of the crowd in front of me. Maybe wearing wedge sandals was a bad idea for move-in.

I turn my gaze right toward a set of four buildings and see the blue and yellow sign displaying *De Neve Plaza* next to the face of the Bruin mascot. I and a few other freshmen push our way out of the river of people who continue to walk up the hill and make our way to the central check-in booth in the plaza of the four unknown buildings. I look toward my left at the largest building out of the four, with two large dorm buildings connecting to a central building.

I glance quickly toward my right at the other two buildings, although they appear a lot shorter. I keep walking and notice I am moving slightly downward into the plaza, alleviating the weight of my backpack on my shoulders and allowing my suitcase to roll faster. The plaza looks partially sunken as two concrete staircases from the two buildings meet at the bottom with lots of move-in carts lined up against the walls of the concrete barrier that separates the grassy area in front of the buildings. Concrete staircases create a path from the bottom of the plaza up to the dorm buildings. More move-in helpers in bright blue shirts bring more carts from the other side of the plaza lot where the move-in truck is headed. Somewhere in the mass of carts is mine but it will be a journey to find it. I get closer to the booth, my heels stinging even more. I just want to move in already.

Finally, I approach the central booth, fanning myself with my free hand, hoping to cool down from the heat. A blonde lady greets me, her smile contagious. "Hi, there! Which building are you moving into?"

"It's uh—" I catch my breath and pull my phone out of my pocket, checking my email for the building name. Dogwood.

"It's D 223," I say while reading it from my phone.

"Perfect!" she exclaims in an enthusiastic tone. "Let me see your Bruin Card."

I pull my student ID from the pocket on the back of my phone and hand it to her. I really hope it's not drenched in my sweat. She swipes my card on the scanner next to a computer and taps on the keyboard. "Alrighty," she responds. "So, you're going to head up the elevator in Dogwood, which is the building right behind me. Let me get your cart really quick."

A few more clicks, then she writes something on a Post-It and walks over to the crowd of move-in carts. She checks the tags of all the carts, glancing at the Post-It. Within a few minutes, she locates another cart, reads the tag, and nods. I notice the large, pink pillow ready to topple over as she pulls the cart from one of the rows. She pushes the cart toward me lightly, then returns to the booth, clicking and typing on the computer. She takes another Post-It, writes something.

"You're all set, hon." She hands me my ID with a post-it stuck to it. "You'll just take the ramp right off the side. One of our move-in assistants will help you carry all this." She calls to one of the people in bright blue shirts. "And the Post-It is the code to access the door with your Bruin Card."

"Awesome, thanks." I put my Bruin Card in my jeans pocket and begin walking, staring at my housing email with the room.

"What building is it again?" one of the helpers asks.

I look up just in time before I bump into the cart, almost losing a grip on my phone. "Dogwood, Room 223." I take a quick glance at the tall, dark-haired man. He seems... *Okay, not now.*

I return to looking back at my phone, trying to read all the housing guidelines sent in an email, even though multitasking might not be the best idea. I keep up with his pace as we near the ramp, heading toward the dorm building.

We arrive in the lobby, which pretty much has the entrance door, the elevator on our right side, a water fountain, and a hallway leading toward the back. I look up at the elevator, waiting for it to open. I find it awkward talking to the guy helping me, partly because I am naturally shy but mostly because I am all over the place trying to understand this new experience. The door opens, and we enter the elevator. I try to catch my breath while staring up at the elevator lights.

"So, I'm guessing you're a freshman, right?"

I look toward the guy, noticing his square-framed glasses and light brown eyes. I always notice the eyes first. "Yeah."

"Oh, me too," he replies.

"Really?" I ask in surprise.

"Yeah. I did that early move-in thing to help out."

"Oh, that makes total sense," I say as the elevator stops, nearly knocking my balance off.

The doors open, and I step out with my suitcase. The guy follows me as I notice another room to my right. This must be the study lounge. I return my gaze forward, noticing a dorm room, a hallway stretching on either side, revealing more rooms. I look up at the first room. Large white letters read 223. Perfect.

"Awesome." I reach for my ID, place it in the card slot, and type in the code. With a click, the door unlocks. I open the door and enter. There's a mini hallway opening to a room with two bunk beds. I see someone on the bottom bunk.

"Hey, roommate!" A girl with blond hair and black streaks gets up from her bed and greets me. "Oh, let me move my stuff. " She grabs her boots from the floor and moves them on her bed as the guy pushes the cart into the room.

Seeing how the cart takes up a lot of space makes me realized how small the dorm is. I turn and see the loft bunk bed is ready for me. I roll my suitcase over to the desk and place my backpack down.

"Awesome," I say to myself. I glance up at the guy, almost forgetting he helped me. "Thank you so much... uh."

"Will."

"Okay, cool. Thanks again."

"Yeah, no problem," he says as he turns to go. "You can return the cart to the same place you got it. They'll take care of it there."

"Oh, right. Thanks."

He walks out of the dorm, the door closing behind him. I take a sigh of relief.

"If you need help with your stuff, let me know," says my roommate as I begin to unload my things from the cart. I take a quick glance at her. Her blond hair is streaked with dark black hues, with prominent dark black and neon green shadow, and her outfit is black from head to toe. Interesting fashion choice.

"Uh, yeah, can you help get the printer out? There's so much stuff in there," I say while unloading my large pillow and bag with my bedding. She reaches in and grabs the printer, setting it on top of my dresser.

"Oh, totally forgot. I'm Madison by the way," she says while helping me unload more bags from the cart.

"Oh, nice to meet you, Madison!" I reply while throwing my bedding on the top bunk. I'll deal with it later.

"I am Curanda."

"Randa?" she asks.

"No, it's Curanda. Just think of cur then anda."

"Cur-anda," she pronounces slowly. It doesn't sound as great with an English accent as it does with a Spanish one but this works.

"Yep. You got it."

"Wow. That's such a cool name. Unique even."

This is the moment that changed my life forever.

CHAPTER 1

PRESENT DAY: SEPTEMBER 28TH, 2018: SECOND YEAR AT UCLA
11 a.m.

Introduction to Abnormal Psychology. The bright yellow heading catches my eye as I glance over the soon-to-be highlighted text on top of three other textbooks in my stack. It's going to be a hard quarter but a good one, for sure. I flip open the textbook, ready to skim it. Even though it seems like a lot, being in psychology is a lot better than trying to be a doctor. It's way more interesting and less intense than pre-med. Suddenly, I hear the click from the door. I glance up and see a blue and yellow move-in cart entering the dorm.

"Hey, Cur!" Madison exclaims, slightly muffled by the pile of pillows and blankets nearly falling off the cart.

"Hey, Maddy!" I push my textbooks farther back on my desk, leaning back to allow Maddy as much space to unload her stuff.

"Need help with that?" I ask.

Maddy finally gets the cart into the center of the room. She glances at me really quick. "Oh, yeah. Thanks." She grabs the largest pillow from the top pile. I am finally able to see her, and she looks so... different. There's no more black streaks in her hair, no bright neon green with black eye shadow, or even her notorious platform Doc Marten boots she always wore. Instead, she's completely blond, covered in what looks like designer clothes: a pink polka dot skirt with white *LV* letters in the dots, a button-up white blouse, round pink sunglasses, and bright pink platform boots. She looked like a model straight out of *Vogue* magazine.

I've always known she had wealthy family back in England, given her family's involvement in politics, but she always said how much she hated the whole pseudo royal look. *"They all just want to be like the Royal Family. Pathetic."*

Yet, that is exactly what she is wearing now. *What happened to Madison?*

"Wow that's a bit of a change." I grab a bag with her comforter in it, briefly noticing its bright pink color.

"What change?" she asks while placing a white box on her desk.

I pull out another white box. "Your whole outfit. Thought you hated the whole 'fancy look,'" I say with air quotes.

She shrugs while reaching in the cart, grabbing another box. "My family pretty much forced it upon me." She places the box on top of the growing stack of boxes on her desk. "Told me I should embrace the 'privilege' you know, coming from a wealthy family and all. I just said 'Hey, why not?'"

"Huh," I say with a slight shrug. *This doesn't sound right.*

I pull the final box out before the last, yet heaviest, thing in there: the printer. We both reach in and pull it out, placing it on her dresser. "I think that's it for now." She takes a brief look at all her piles of boxes needing to be unpacked "Oh, can you take the cart out so I can unload?"

"Sure thing." I push the empty cart out of the room, heading toward the elevators. It reminds me of last year, when I first moved into this dorm building and here I am a year later doing the same thing. I just can't believe how much a year can change you, especially with Madison. Something is fishy, and it doesn't seem right. Or I could just be overthinking things.

12 p.m.

I return from the move-in cart trek and open the door.

"Hey," I say while closing the door behind me and heading to my textbooks piled desk.

"Hey, Cur." Madison looks at her bright LED vanity mirror as she puts mascara on.

"You're going somewhere?" I look around at the dorm. My eyes widen in shock. Her comforter is no longer the vibrant purple galaxy pattern with a pentagram in the middle. Instead, it is hot pink with a Louis Vuitton pattern accompanied by pink and white furry pillows.

"No. Just needed to touch up my makeup." She continues to look intently into the mirror.

"That's... cool." I catch a glimpse of her desk. She has designer perfumes and a makeup case embedded with diamonds. Even her backpack hanging on her chair has black *LV* letters against a gold glittery pattern. Before it was a plain ole black backpack and none of those things on her desk. Nor was she so fixated on her makeup as she is now.

"Yeah. I need it to be perfect, you know. It looks so much better when it is." She stops angling her face toward the mirror.

"Uh, Maddy?" I suddenly need to know what is going on.

"Yeah." She turns around on her chair.

"Are you sure everything's okay?"

"Yeah everything's fi—"

"I am serious, Maddy," I interject. "This is such a dramatic change from last year."

Maddy's gaze drops the floor where her suitcase lays, unopened. She shakes her head. "This is the true me, you know. I thought the dark look was what I wanted because my family appeared to be the snooty rich stereotype but, in all honesty…" She gets up from her chair, glances at her nails, extending her fingers up, the glittery colors shining, then meeting my gaze. "I love this look. Sophistication, royalty." She walks over to the bathroom door, staring at herself in the mirror, smiling. "I should've embraced it long ago."

I am lost for words. The old Maddy would be sickened hearing this; would hate the type of makeup that makes women look like Kylie Jenner. She glances at me for a second then opens the bathroom door. I lean against my desk, my thoughts racing a mile a minute trying to figure out why she's changed so much. *This isn't the Maddy I know.*

I hear the bathroom cabinet door open. "Perfect," Maddy says as she closes the door and walks out, tossing a box on her desk. I eye the box, my eyes widening. *Yep. That's what I think it is.*

"Um… do you have a date tonight?" I ask.

"Yeah, about that." She opens her desk drawer, revealing her glittery pink iPhone. She scrolls and types out a message then turns to me.

"I am gonna need the dorm tonight, around nine tonight until midnight. I'm meeting someone I met from Tinder, and we are going to be busy, for sure."

"Well, that's a little late and I was hoping to unpack the rest of my stuff. Maybe tomor—"

"Cur!" she interjects. "You've always been okay with it before. Why can't you let me tonight?"

"You always tell me beforehand and have never done it during move-in weekend so it's odd that—"

"Wow." She puts her phone on her desk and rolls her eyes. "So, you're not going to let me have the dorm?"

I am in shock. I hate confrontation but I have to stand my ground. "No, Maddy, you can't. I still haven't unpacked some boxes from the closet and I need—"

"I don't care about your boxes, Cur. I finally meet someone worthwhile on Tinder and now you're going to ruin it for me all for just a few boxes?" She shakes her head in disbelief and stares out the window.

"Maddy, I am tired, I still have way more to unpack. The max I can do is about an hour but that's—"

"I can't believe you, Cur." She crosses her arms in front of her. "When you had your friends over until midnight last quarter, I never had a problem with it."

"Yeah, because that didn't happen during move-in weekend, and we were all okay with it. You and Karen were part of those hangouts, and I still gave you two a heads-up beforehand."

"Unbelievable." She takes off her platform boots and tosses them across the dorm, close to my bed. "Guess I am not going anywhere." She continues taking off her earrings and necklace and throws them on her desk. I can feel the tension; the air in the room getting heated.

"Well, can't you go over to his place?" I ask.

She shakes her head. "I can't cause he lives up in Hedrick." *Is she really making a ten-minute walk not worth her time?*

"Um, Hedrick is not that far. It's not like an apartment—"

"I refuse to walk up the literal hill to stay in a smaller, hot ass room. No," she says.

"But you're okay kicking me out, knowing that I need this place just for your enjoyment?"

"That's about right."

What. The. Hell.

"What happened to you?" I ask.

"What happened to *you*, Cur?" she says sarcastically. "You were so chill last year. Now you're controlling— "

"I am not controlling at all. I just know our boundaries that we created last year to make sure we'd get along—"

"Oh, that's wonderful. Boundaries." She meets my gaze. "Guess we need new boundaries, don't we?"

"I—"

"No." She shakes her head while walking over to the body mirror on the bathroom door. "Don't be surprised if you walk in on us tonight," she says with a chuckle right as she's about to enter the bathroom. *I have had enough.*

"Honestly, I don't know what crawled up your ass and died, but I am not leaving this dorm just so you can get some dick!" I exclaim. "I still have a lot of unpacking to do. And if we are already having problems now, I don't think it's going to get better later on."

"Wow, Cur." She turns around and I catch a glimpse of the cabinet full of beauty products. *Dear God.* "Looks like someone's jealous," she says with a grin.

"Jealous? You honestly think I am jealous of you? I would never think that. What I'm saying is that you're being completely unreasonable!"

"Curanda, Curanda, Curanda," she says, shaking her head. "Looks like we're going to have issues, aren't we?" She storms past me, grabbing her shoes off the floor and walks over to her closet, pulling out a pink LV strap purse. She grabs her phone and shoves it into the purse while I move to take a step back from her chaos.

"I have somewhere to be. Have fun unpacking," she says sarcastically as she walks out, slamming the door behind her.

I shake my head, staring at the carpet, feeling my heartbeat fast in my chest. I never thought my best friend would just completely change. We never fought like this before. We used to be the best of friends—we did everything together and even showed each other our powers, nearly scaring Karen to death.

> "Hey, Cur?" whispers Maddy from across the dorm. She meets my eyes then gestures down to Karen's desk, peeking her head over the bedframe of the bunk. I know that sign. She wants me to show my powers. Karen's never seen them before, and her succulent she loved so much was sitting dark brown and withered in its pot on her desk. She's going to freak out. She's putting Post-Its on her desk, scribbled with notes, just above the succulent.
>
> Maddy looks back at me, nodding. I close my eyes, placing my right hand in front of me near my face, concentrating all my power on the plant, feeling a rush of energy and euphoria, tingling from my head down to my toes, my body pulsing with energy. Any minute now.
>
> "What the fuck?" Karen says quickly. "Oh, my. Oh, my. Holy shit!" she screams. A loud thump awakens me from my channeling of energy. I open my eyes. Maddy is giggling on her bunk.
>
> "Karen, what's going—" Maddy leans over as I look toward her desk, seeing the succulent's withered form turn bright

green, its circular leaves filling with water. "Oh, shit," Maddy says enthusiastically. Karen had knocked her chair over and was trembling in the hallway, her hands covering her face. Oh, no. Maddy and I climb down the bunk.

Karen is sobbing and trembling. She points to the succulent. "That shit was dead this morning. I—I... " she stutters. "I saw it grow back with my own fucking eyes." Karen starts breathing faster, her trembling becoming more intense. Karen's going into full panic-mode.

"Karen... Karen..." Maddy says as she meets Karen's tear-filled gaze. "Keep looking at me, hun, Okay?" Karen nods, her body slowly sinking to the floor. Maddy and I crouch down, comforting her. "Okay, I want you to look around and find five things you see. Can you do that?" Maddy asks.

Karen glances at her, then the ceiling and around the dorm. Maddy whispers something under her breath while Karen looks around. She instantly stops trembling; her breathing starts slowing down to its normal pace. Must be her healing spell.

Her breathing returns to normal as she stares at her desk. "You guys saw it, right?"

"We did," I reply as I push her desk chair back, noticing the excellent job I did at the unfortunate expense of Karen's sanity.

"What... what happened?" she asks us.

I sigh. "You promise not tell anyone, okay?"

Karen looks up at me, sniffling. "I promise."

Now it's like she's a stranger, someone I never knew nor want to know anymore. I shake my head, bringing myself back to reality, and reach for my phone, messaging Leo in the process. He's one of my best friends who should've moved in by now. He might also want Anna to join us as well. We call ourselves the notorious trio as we all met in the same summer program right before our freshman year. We've been hanging out as much as we could, given how hard UCLA is, but we manage to find the time to do so. Finally, I hear a ding.

```
Sure. Let's bring Anna too. I'll message
her right now.
```

Perfect. I definitely need some down time. After a few minutes, I decide to take a brief walk outside, wanting to get my mind off this situation. I walk down the stairs and play some good ole *Avicii* to relax me. I love EDM so much. It allows me to escape this hectic world by just taking a break. As I reach the bottom of the stairs, ready to embark on my short walk around the hill, Leo responds.

```
We're at B plate. Wanted to get a booth.
Come join us.
```

Ah, B Plate. The best dining hall on campus. Well, at least, to me since I am vegetarian and love all the healthy options they have. It's my go-to for all my food if I am not in a rush. I missed this dining hall so much. Having spent two months in an apartment this past summer made me cherish food that is made for me and not by me. I walk on the curvy path behind my dorm building. It's a little shortcut that's lined with flowers but has some pine trees that throw off some annoying little branches that I slip on all the time. Still, this shortcut reminds me to stay present.

I reach the crosswalk leading up to the staircase that I have to climb to get to the dining hall. Again, it's a lot of work but totally worth it. Finally, I reach the front kiosk and hand the lady behind the counter my card, who then swipes me in for an endless buffet of healthy food. I pull out my phone, ready to text Leo, when I hear Anna's voice.

"Hey, Cur!" She speed walks up to me but can't give me hug since she's carrying like four plates in her hand.

"Hey, Anna! Wow, that's a lot of plates."

"Yeah. You accumulate a lot here as always," she says with a laugh. "We're in the back by the cereal. Come, I'll show you," she says while guiding me to their spot.

I pass by the endless tables that crowd the center, filled with lots of students who had just moved in, talking up a storm about how their summer went and how they've missed B plate. It's just a cacophony of endless conversations. I miss this feeling despite my social-anxiety-prone ass.

Normally, I'd just zone this out but since it's been so long since I've actually been here, it's comforting. I pass by the pizza station, followed by the drink station all the way to the back. The booth is pretty much this long bench with tables stacked in front of it. It's the most popular spot though. My guess is it's because you're close to all the food, but I am not too sure. For me at least, it gives me a break from that loud mess in the center of the dining hall.

We reach our table that's almost covered in stacks of plates but also good-looking food. Although I am vegetarian, the salmon is good, which I know from my pescatarian days. So, there's loads of salmon on the table. And since Leo's gone, he's probably in line for something else. I remember the spot and go to all the vegetation stations, which have virtually no line. Pretty soon I had a stack of plates like Leo and Anna. I head back to our spot and find Leo and Anna scarfing down their salmon and Brussels sprouts while I dig into my vegan poké bowl and three pieces of grilled tofu.

Finally, once we were all stuffed with food, the conversation starts.

"So, how was your summer, Cur?" Leo asks while adjusting his wired frame glasses.

I take a sip of tea to clear my throat. "My summer was great. I did research in my new addiction lab. Got to take care of rats and I even had my own apartment, which probably wasn't the best choice food-wise. But yeah. It was pretty chill."

"That's good. Pretty cool research though, right?" Leo asks.

I nod. "It's too advanced for undergrads to understand but I get the gist of it. Plus, I had to make my own research poster about all of the data." I take another sip. "Now that I got experience, I honestly don't think this whole research thing may be my thing after all, so I'll figure what to do next."

"How about you, Anna? Do anything exciting this summer?" Leo looks at Anna, who just took a large bite of salmon right as he asked her that.

She tries to chew as fast as she can, leaving that semi-awkward silence amongst us, but once I giggle, Anna smiles. "My summer was pretty chill. I got an internship at a local marketing business near my house. Made me realized how hard marketing and business are. Might change my major from business to something else but we'll see," she says while drinking her soda. "What about you, Leo?"

"Well," he says, looking at the napkin holder at the center of the table. "It was pretty uneventful. Just spent the whole time at my grandmother's. But I did some reading to prep for this quarter. That alien, psychics, and ghost class along with the creative writing class is gonna be a lot of reading and writing."

"Wait," I say as realization dawned on me. "Are you in English 20w? That's creative writing, I think?"

He nods. "The one with Anderson, right? The morning seminar?"

"Yeah. I'm taking that class!" I exclaim. "Dude, we can so study together." I am so thankful for Leo. He's kind of the nerd in our trio who loves to prepare ahead of time. Very on top of his stuff, unlike me. He is *so* gonna save me in that class.

"We definitely should cause it's gonna be a lot of work. I'm just gonna be so busy academic-wise. It's already stressing me out," says Leo.

"Same!" Anna and I say at the exact moment.

"How about we not talk about school, yet," Leo says while I take one last sip of my water. "Hey, Cur. How's Maddy? I haven't heard from her at all."

I shake my head and sigh. "She's a mess."

"What?" Leo asks with a confused expression. "What happened?"

"We got into an argument over her wanting the dorm for three hours just to bring a Tinder date over."

"What the hell?" Anna says while drinking her tea.

"Yeah that's... different," says Leo.

I nod. "Then on top of that, her whole persona changed. I don't know what the hell happened, but she did a complete 180 this summer."

"Wait," says Anna. "Does she still wear the kickass goth makeup?"

I shake my head. "Let me tell you how much she's changed: She has *Louis Vuitton* bedding."

Anna and Leo look at each other, then at me. "No way," Leo replies.

"Yeah. She's turned into those stereotypical rich kids, even though she always hated the look."

"She was never like that before," says Anna while taking in the news. "How bad is this entitlement?"

"I am considering meeting with the RA tonight or tomorrow hoping to get some more conflict resolution skills. I never had to meet with them for any problem last year. Not even when Karen brought over her mean sorority sister."

"What the…" Anna stares down at the napkin holder.

I nod, taking a sip of a little water from my melted ice. "Yeah. This move-in and Maddy. It's all a mess."

"Shit," Anna says while fiddling with her fork.

"Cur, if you ever need a place to stay, my suite mates wouldn't mind at all if you take the couch," Leo says with a look of concern.

"I so wish we could be roomies, but I know you don't like the community bathroom in my building," says Anna.

"It's fine. I will manage this somehow," I reply.

"Wait. Is she still a witch considering she's had this drastic change?" Leo asks.

I shrug. "I have no idea. I'm pretty sure she still is though. She comes from a line of famous witches, of course, under the guise of rich politicians, but I'm sure she's keeping up with the tradition."

"Hmm," says Leo while looking in the distance.

"That's so weird how fast she changed," says Anna.

"I know. It sucks because I was hoping to learn more from her witch side. I don't know if her new rich girl identity will erase that," I say while delving into my thoughts, leaving all of us quiet for a moment. That's when I remembered something. I plan on heading to Aura Vita, my safe haven but also cool metaphysical store back home. Just to relieve some stress, but I know Leo wanted to go.

"Hey, Leo," I say while looking in his direction. He turns to me, his gaze returning to mine. "I am going to my spiritual store and I know you've wanted to go for the longest time. Want to go with me tomorrow morning?"

"What time?"

"We'll leave around eleven and spend the afternoon there. Plus, I got to pick up some stuff from my house. You can meet Lucy, my go-to for spiritual things."

He nods. "I'll more than likely be up at six anyways, so that works."

"Perfect! I'll drive us."

"You got a car?" Anna asks with wide eyes.

I nod. "My parents decided it was time I have one. They surprised me with it at the start of summer."

"That's so cool!" exclaims Anna.

"How did you manage to get a parking spot? I heard it's so hard to get one while in the dorms?" Leo asks.

"I pleaded real hard with UCLA to give me a spot. Lots of paperwork but totally worth it."

"That's awesome," replies Leo.

"Girl, you better take me to the beach sometime!" exclaims Anna.

I nod. "I promise I will take you both before late fall hits. Just don't expect a fancy ride."

"What kind of car do you have?" asks Leo.

"It's very basic. It's two years old but it has roll-up windows and no Bluetooth. That already tells you a lot."

"Oh, my God," Anna says with a chuckle. "I guess any car is better than no car, right?"

I nod. "Oh, yeah, I just dread the traffic I have to face going from West LA to the Eastside. That's not going to be fun but it's worthwhile to get a break from move-in and all. I never thought I'd actually have to avoid her during move-in, but hey. Life, I guess."

"Okay. Let's all head back and finish unpacking." I turn to Leo. "I'll send you a message tomorrow before I take off. Oh, Anna. Do you want to come with us?"

She shakes her head as we begin to pick up our stacks of plates to drop them off at the cleaning station before we leave. "I would but my roommates wanted to have lunch in Westwood. So, I'll be with them all day tomorrow," she says as we drop off our plates on the conveyor belt.

I hate parting ways. I so do not want to go back to my dorm, but I do want to sleep early and, hopefully, get some good sleep. We all say goodbye as we head off in totally different directions. Anna heads upstairs to her dorm, Leo heads down the other staircase leading north, and I head down the third staircase heading back to De Neve.

I return to the dorm building, opening the door and heading up the stairs, hoping to get back to unpack all of my things. I reach the second floor and feel my phone vibrate in my jean shorts pocket. I open the phone, receiving a text from Maddy.

```
Busy with the dorm. I'll tell you when I
am done.
```

"You've got to be kidding me!" I exclaim with a sigh. I shake my head and lean against the wall near the lounge. I pick up my phone again and call Leo.

"Hey, Leo."

"Hey, Cur. What's up?"

I look toward my dorm door, shaking my head in disbelief. "I am actually going to need a place to stay for the night."

SEPTEMBER 29TH, 2018
11:11 a.m.

I park my car in Aura Vita's parking lot, which I've known so well from working here part-time back in high school. It's been a few months since I've visited due to being away at UCLA plus doing a research program over this summer. I've learned that research is not my strong suit, and I am so thankful for food in the dorms. I am so not the best cook in an apartment. Plus, I almost forgot about Leo in the backseat. He fell asleep at some point of the drive. I open the back door, tap him on the shoulder, and he wakes up.

"We're here. Come check this place out," I say while letting him get out of the car. He closes the door and follows me down the sidewalk. We walk around building toward the front, where the sign Aura Vita in neon orange greets me.

I open the front door and instantly smell the musk of sandalwood incense, the giant cauldron full of crystals greeting me. I remember the first time coming here, when Lucy introduced me to crystals and stones. She showed me that same cauldron.

> *Lucy picks up a small purple stone from the rainbow of crystals. "This is called amethyst." She places it in my palm that's coated with sweat out of nervousness. "It's known for its abilities to connect to the spirit realm."*

I still have that same amethyst, placed in a small velvet bag in my backpack.

I look toward the center of store where a large golden statue of Ganesh still remains. Incense sticks are placed around him and money placed at his feet. That sign is still there, the one that says *Stealing from the saints is bad luck* scrawled in black marker. Behind Ganesh is a table with buckets holding numerous incense sticks; each of the six buckets are filled with different scents and sizes. So, if you wanted a two-foot long incense stick, here's the place to get it. Beneath the buckets are shelves that have other spiritual things like an old-fashioned incense holder, camphor cubes, Palo Santo, white sage, and smoking pipes.

On the left side wall lies the candle section. This one is my favorite even though I used to be so scared restocking the shelves since they're all made of glass and I *so* did not want to break the candles since they cost a fortune to replace. It's just that there's *so* many of them. It's like two library sections filled with candles from all the zodiac signs and even ones for love, good luck, and prosperity. There's so many more! I am just happy to have my libra candle and my good luck candle for career/work-related things.

Next to the candle section is the front register with the glass case behind it that houses the crystals. These are like clear quartz charms for jewelry or even bracelets made of intricate stones and wiring that makes it cost a fortune since it's all handmade. I bought a clear quartz necklace three years ago and I still wear it.

Toward the back of the store is the curtain laden arch. I call it the "brujas cave." This is where things get interesting. Behind that curtain is an entirely different world. Most people aren't allowed back there since they don't have powers like Lucy and I do. Only those who have powers can see light glow behind the curtains. Lucy told me it's a protective barrier from other magical beings or people who wish to do harm. It also prevents people from seeing the magic behind the scenes that Lucy does for clients, some of which are psychic readings, candle preparations, and spiritual cleanses. Lucy still advises me to stay away from the back until I am comfortable and ready to explore that whole realm of magic.

Let me explain. The psychic readings involve the main owner of the shop doing a tarot reading, clairvoyant reading, and energy healing all in one. This is done in a small room off the side of the register behind the dark brown wooden door that has a sign hanging from it with the phrase *Reading in Progress* written in scrawled black letters next to picture of a purple crystal ball. When going in for a reading, they can tell you about your future, what you are feeling now, and how to overcome or handle things you have been having problems with.

In a candle prep, they have you write your name a few times and your intention for your candle. They then take it to the back and the rest is pretty much a mystery. And spiritual cleanses are somewhat confusing to me, but I've heard they get an egg, wave it around your body, and then crack it to take away negative energy or vibes you may be experiencing. These are also held in the same small room where the readings are held.

The other side of the store contains shelves of oils, boxes, spiritual tools like wands, herbs to burn based on your intention, more jewelry, tapestries, and books. And these books aren't your ordinary ones. They are about Wicca, Tarot, Santeria Kabbalah, mysticism—you name it, it's there. So yeah, this store is pretty amazing. I remember when I told Lucy about that glowing light behind the curtain. She was in shock and asked me to describe it more. That same day, I told her about my power and showed her its potential. I knew I was different when I first found out my powers when I was about eight years old. My parents used to fight a lot, so I spent most of my time outside in the backyard admiring all the beautiful flowers. One flower caught my eye as I looked at the faint pink petals that were starting to wilt. I wanted to see the color come back. I touched the flower with the desire of it to return and it slowly began to rise, its petals turning bright pink. That's when I knew I was different. And no one in my family had powers at all given how important religion was. I knew I couldn't show this to anyone.

She commended my power, but she still thinks I can enhance it or discover more of what I am capable of. She already told me that I am an empath, which is someone who is capable of feeling a lot of emotions from other people. We're pretty much like emotional sponges and no, we don't do it voluntarily. It happens without conscious control. So, Lucy had given me advice on how to handle that. I've gotten stones that I carry with me, incense that I burn to make me feel at ease and burn herbs when I feel the need to.

It's just so hard to do it when I live in a dorm. That's why these essential oils will save me. Or I can just not abide by dorm rules and burn it anyway.

"What are you doing here? Aren't you supposed to be at UCLA?" Lucy asks as I pick up a brand new box of seven chakra incense cones. She comes over to where I am shopping and gives me a big hug. She's still wearing her sun and moon cloak that she loves so much; the bright orange sun and moon drawings glow against the black background. She even has her thin wired glasses that almost look like they're going to fall off.

"And is this your boyfriend?" She gestures to Leo.

"Oh, no. He's just a friend. This is Leo," I reply.

"Mmhmm," she says as Leo extends his hand in greeting. She shakes it while looking at Leo. She's analyzing him. "You're an interesting man. You're into the metaphysical, right?" she asks, gesturing to the entire store.

He nods then adjusts his glasses. Right as he was about to speak, Lucy points to the bookshelf. "On the top shelf, the fourth book to the right, there's a book on astral projection. Read it. It'll help guide you on your journey," she says while walking toward the front of the store to replace an incense stick that was burning out.

I've always wanted to be like her: wear her orange and black cloak and have a shop like this. Even though I'll be in a dorm that prohibits incense, I decided that burning this would help me relieve stress, especially since Madison did a complete 180 over summer break in terms of personality and style. I love coming to Aura Vita. It was my home in high school and it's still my favorite place in college. It seems that when things get tough or just hectic, I come here to relax.

"So, you've come here to visit, or do you need something?" she says while igniting the incense stick. "I can sense some tension and maybe something is..." She turns around, her wire-frame glasses at the bridge of her nose "...off?"

I nod. "I've got a problem," I say as I fill my shopping basket with more incense cones. "My roommate has changed completely. Like did a complete 180 and is already causing problems."

"Is this your bruja friend who bought the book of spells?" *Oh, yeah, I totally forgot Lucy has met Madison.*

"Yeah, she's the one who comes from the witch family in England." Maddy's family initially appears to be these rich politicians that produce the next generation of Prime

Ministers of England, but hidden behind those rich appearances is the fact that her family is part of a long line of powerful witches that spans thousands of years.

Her father, Raymond Scar, is the most powerful warlock in all of Europe while her mother is the most powerful witch in England. That entire family has power and riches oozing from their veins, in both the mortal and magical realms. Maddy used to hate that rich persona her family touts in England along with the continual corruption involved with politics. She hated all the drama, all the wealth and constant fame her family dealt with all the time. She decided to move here to get away from all that and take on a new persona with her dark goth witch look.

But now, she's totally different.

"Ah, yes," she says, lost in thought for a moment. "To be honest, she seemed like a good person, but something was off about her."

"Clearly, since she's so mean," I reply while gathering two bottles of essential oils. Citrus and Gardenia, my favorites.

"She's mean?" asks Lucy.

"She's *really* mean and it's bad. She expects me to give her everything she wants. She kicked me out of our dorm last night so I had to stay with my friend. She's also sporting all designer clothes too. She looks like one of the preppy girls from my high school," I spill all of this, desperate to find answers to this dilemma.

Lucy nods then stares off in the distance, mumbling something in Spanish. She looks up and heads across the store toward the candle section.

"You're gonna need protection," she says suddenly as she reaches for a black candle. I've never liked black candles since they seem so scary. Like who just randomly has an all-black candle?

Plus, this candle scares me even more with the picture of death on it, hooded and robed with the sickle and all. I never liked protection candles. I just don't understand why this one.

"Protection? From what? Her petty attitude?" I say, surprised that I would ever need this candle. Lucy gives me a serious look. I've never seen that look on her face when she prepared my candles.

Uh oh.

"I am gonna prepare this candle for you. And you're gonna need a black tourmaline stone bracelet. I'll prepare it as—"

"Lucy, I can't afford all this," I interrupt. My budget is only about twenty dollars and that's it. Both things are a lot more than that.

"You're gonna need this. Trust me," she says while retrieving little sheets of paper for both the bracelet and candle.

"You know the drill, right?" she asks, heading over to the jewelry cabinet to retrieve an all-black stone bracelet.

I nod. "Write your name seven times and carve your name inside the candle, not too close to the wick. Write my name eight times for the bracelet and intentions on the back of each sheet, right?"

She nods. "Yep. Good girl. And for the intention, you can write anything, but protection of some form is highly recommended."

"Will do," I say as I write my name for the candle prep.

I write my intentions down and Lucy takes everything to the bruja's cave. I've gotten candles before to represent my zodiac sign and one for luck in school, both of which were benign intention-based magic. I never liked the black candles due to their intimidating appearance and the fact that they can be used for evil when placed in the wrong hands. I know this candle prep will take a few moments. So, I head over to the bookshelf, where Leo decided to sit and read *Astral Travel: The Basics*.

"Did you get to look around the store?" I ask.

He nods. "This is such a peaceful place. And the lady knew exactly what I needed. This book is amazing, and I can't put it down. There's so many other good books too."

"Yeah, I should take a good look at the titles. I hardly ever do," I say while looking at all the other books. Then I see something that catches my attention.

A new pack of tarot cards.

Lucy is totally fine with her customers exploring the decks, and since no one else decided to come on a Saturday afternoon to the store, I decided to open the deck. I have always hesitated using tarot cards since I have heard that they are powerful. My family used to say that I might also bring demons or something in my house due to the Catholic propaganda from my parents. But I don't know why something keeps drawing me in, like a moth to a flame. Due to this hidden fear, Lucy introduced me to oracle cards, which are pretty much just motivational messages. She calls it the "nicer cousin of the tarot," as you can get oracle cards themes ranging from angels to Nature Spirits.

So, I have an angel oracle deck that I was able to use back at home. My parents thought I was making a stronger connection to God and the angels with it but in reality, I was trying to use them similar to tarot cards. Needless to say, it didn't work well. I grab the box named *Quick and Easy Tarot* and open it, revealing an orange background for the cards. I shuffle the deck and decide to ask it something.

"Well, tarot cards, what message do I need to know?" I ask it and pull a random card from the deck.

I turn the card over. And I see a lovely crescent moon with wolves howling at it.

"Hmm. That's cool," I say. Thank God this tarot deck is easy to understand with descriptions written at the top of the cards.

Something in your life is not what it seems. Perhaps a misunderstanding on your part, or a truth you cannot admit to yourself. It may also indicate something important being kept from you by another. This may be a source of worry or depression in your life, and the Moon is a strong indicator that you must rely on your intuition to see through the subterfuge.

"What the—" I say, confused by the message.

"Curanda, your stuff is ready!" Lucy says as she comes back to the register with all my stuff bagged. Next thing I know, Lucy heads over to the bookshelf, shocked at the tarot cards.

"Curanda," Lucy says as she stares at the card in my hand then at me. "That's your deck."

"My deck?" I ask, still confused.

"From what I can tell, that tarot deck is accurate. I want you to be protected. My intuition tells me that Madison has something hidden and it's not good. There's not much else I can say."

"I thought I couldn't read tarot decks. I don't have powers aside from my green thumb," I say, confused as ever.

"Curanda," Lucy says while glancing at the moon card then back to me. "Take the deck. Whenever you feel lost, confide in it. Don't worry about payment," she says as she heads back to document my purchase.

I put the cards back in the box and take my basket full of incense and oils to the front register. Lucy packs everything into a large paper bag.

"Also, before you go, Cur, I packed you black salt as well. Place it around your living space. And if things get worse…" She swallows awkwardly with a look of worry on her face. I can tell she knows something and it's not good. "Move out. Try to, if things do get worse." She glances at the Ganesh statue.

"I promise I will," I tell her as Leo seems too entrenched in his book.

"But before I go I want you to have this," I say while offering my money to her.

She shakes her head. "It's okay, *mija*. You need these for your own safety and well-being. You can give this offering to the saints." She looks up at the Ganesh statue. I nod and walk over to the statue, placing my twenty-dollar bill among the stack of coins and dollars in the box by the feet.

"Leo," I call to him. He looks up. "We gotta go," I say while walking back to the register and picking up my bag.

Lucy walks over to Leo, noticing the book in his hands as he gets up from the floor. He places the book back on the shelf as Lucy approaches. "*Mijo,* you can keep the book," she says while giving it back to Leo.

"Also, one more thing," she says while walking over to the glass case with all the pendulums and necklaces. She picks up a necklace with a purple pendant in the shape of a donut tied with black string. She hands it to Leo, who is mesmerized by the necklace.

"That is pure amethyst. It'll act as both a protective amulet and also enhance your intuition. You can wear it or just keep it with you on your journey," she says with a smile.

Leo is speechless. He reaches into his pocket, about to hand her some money. "I need to pay you this. I can't just leave without—"

"Don't," she says while cupping his hand. "You are gifted with something so powerful. Use the book and this amulet to help you discover that gift. If you want to make an offering, place it at the feet of Ganesh just as Cur did."

Leo nods. "Thank you so much," he replies and walks over to the Ganesh statue, placing his money in the box below his feet.

"Thanks for everything, Lucy," I say as we reach the door.

"You're welcome, *mija,* and nice meeting you, Leo," she says as we walk out of the store, carrying our bags.

As soon as we're in my car, I place my bag into the passenger seat, making sure to place the plastic bag with the candles gently on the floor, otherwise the oil will cause another stain like last time. I reach into the bag and pull out my bracelet, noticing the darkness within the round, polished stones. I roll it on my left wrist and reach for the tarot box in my bag and open it.

"Wow, Lucy is so cool. I can't believe she gave me this…" Leo starts talking about the books and his necklace, but I am too entrenched in my tarot cards to hear what he's saying.

"One more thing, Mr. Tarot," I say as I shuffle the cards in my hand. "What should I look forward to this quarter?" I turn over the card and see a giant goblet of some sort.

"Ace of cups, what do you mean?" I ask while reading the description at the top.

> *Intense friendships. Loving family. Joy and peace. The beginning of great love. Follow your heart and your instincts. Let your guard down and open your heart. You can trust this person. You will find your soulmate. Count on your friends."*

"My soulmate? Sure," I say as I place the cards back in the box and into the paper bag.

"Curanda." Leo brings me back to reality.

"Yeah. Sorry. I got lost in the tarot cards," I say as I turn over the driver seat to meet his gaze. "What's up?" I ask while seeing him buried in his book.

"The Astral Projection book says I can engage in multidimensional jumping. I can go from this current world to other worlds out in the universe!" he exclaims.

"That is pretty cool," I say while thinking about that. "Also, do you want to sit in the front?"

He shakes his head. "I might want to nap during the traffic jam, so I'll lay back here."

"Okay. Cool." I turn on the ignition. I still can't get my mind off the card I pulled in the store. I shake my head and shift my mind into driving mode.

Have I really been warned?

CHAPTER 2

OCTOBER 9TH, 2018

"Hey, have you reached the end yet?" Leo asks while I make a quick note about the story. I look up from my notebook, shake my head, and meet his gaze. I underestimated Virginia Woolf's essay.

"She keeps describing how insignificant the moth is compared to humanity. And honestly, I am not going to reach the end anytime soon. Can you tell me what the last line is? It'll save me so much time."

"Sure, of course," he says while pushing his square-framed glasses up the bridge of his nose.

I didn't think that this creative writing class would be so demanding. Yet here I am, during the first week of classes, stuck with about three hours' worth of reading material.

I am barely on the third story out of five that we have to read. I am just thankful that we were able to get the best study space in all of UCLA: a private lounge in the basement of the library. Has a whiteboard and all. It's the perfect place to motivate myself to read.

And then, of course, there's Leo, my best friend, who is going to help me ace this class partly because he's a fast reader who loves understanding the deeper meaning of the texts we read. Today's reading is on Virginia Woolf's essay "Death of a Moth."

"So, here's the last line: *'But even as I did so, the unmistakable tokens of death showed themselves. The body relaxed, and instantly grew stiff. The struggle was over. The insignificant little creature now knew death.'*"

"Death of a moth. Ironically starts and ends with the word death," I say while doodling a note on the margins of my notebook: *Moths suck.*

"Hey, do you want to take a break?" Leo asks while readjusting his glasses once more.

I nod while closing my course reader and notebook.

"What should we do now?" he asks.

In the back of my mind, I imagine myself back in my dorm, doing a tarot reading to describe my potential outcome in this class. It would probably give me the tower, which is the worst card to have because it means destruction and utter failure. Or I can read Leo's cards. I haven't done many readings on my friends since I am a beginner reader, but it would be fun to do that. Maybe he might be up to it.

"Hey, remember those tarot cards I got from my spiritual store?"

He nods. "My mother told me to stay away from it with her being a devout Christian and all. But, like you, I'm the esoteric and mystical arts rebellion of the family. So, I am so not letting her opinion prevent me from getting my hands on them. I don't really know much of what they can do."

"Oh." I glance at the table then meet his gaze. "I thought you knew about them. I just assumed you did since you're into the mystical arts."

He shakes his head. "I have a vague idea about them. That class I took on psychics and ghosts last quarter briefly mentioned them."

"Well, some readings may be like that but—"

"I would love to know…" he interrupts me while holding his chin, staring up at the ceiling. He's thinking about something.

"Know what?" I ask.

He continues staring upward. After a few moments of silence, he meets my eyes. "Bring out your cards, shuffle them, but don't let me see the front side or whatever side has the image. Grab one. I want to see if I can predict the card."

"Alrighty then," I say as I pull out a small red velvet bag with a golden crescent moon logo. It's about the size of a pencil bag, while the deck itself is about the size of a thick stack of Post-Its. I pull out the cards, feeling the smoothness of the cardstock

I gaze at the crisscrossed black and blue stripes that indicate the back of the card. After a few rounds of shuffling, I place the deck face down on the table and fan them out, creating a barrier between us.

I grab one card randomly from the center of the spread, covering it to make sure he doesn't see it. Death, the card I hated the most. The skeleton knight, riding a red-eyed horse while carrying a black flag with a silver flower in the center. It's so... macabre yet beautiful.

The sun shines in the corner over the green hills in the distance. It's small but bright, offering *some* hope. The villagers surrounding Death are on their knees, begging to be spared. Yet Death spares no one. Not even the emperor dressed in gold, full of wealth.

Death is here with a message. I keep my facial expression calm, not giving him any hint of the fear that I feel from seeing this. I place the card face down, making sure those stripes are the only thing visible. "Guess the card."

He leans back for a second, staring up at the ceiling. He starts to look confused. "I see a skull of some sort. No, it's a knight. There's a king offering something, children are by his side. Something's gonna die," he says as he looks down at the cards. I am shocked.

What is dying? When? Should I ask Leo? Wait, Leo has never worked with the cards.

"Leo. Have you ever worked with cards before?"

He shakes his head. "I have seen *some* images but honestly, it's been so long I can't recall that many."

"Well," I say while flipping the card over. "You guessed it spot-on. It makes no sense." I hand him the card.

Leo examines it. His eyes widen in surprise.

"Umm, Leo."

"Yeah."

"You said something is dying or *someone*?"

"Something. I just don't know what. Maybe an animal or insect." He looks off in the distance as a look of realization masks his expression. It's as if a light bulb went on in his mind. "Maybe it's because of the story we just read!"

"That is probably why. 'Death of a Moth' would be fitting!"

"Or I am one pretty good guesser," he says as he returns the card into the deck. "How about we test that out with another card?"

"Okay. Let me shuffle it again for you," I reply.

I shuffle the deck and randomly pick another card, making sure he doesn't see it. Four of Cups. *He'll never get this one.* I place the card face down on the table. "Guess the card."

He rubs his hands together and closes his eyes. It's quiet for a few moments. "I see four golden cups. There's a man sitting by a tree, and some magical hand shrouded in mist holding the last cup. It's as if it's delivering a message to the man. Something about needing retreat or meditation to find oneself considering he's all alone with all these cups that could represent his thoughts."

Again. I am shocked. He is guessing these spot-on; probably even better than I can interpret with three months of practice. He blows me away.

"Yep. Right again." I hand him the card and look up the card description on my phone. I read its meaning out loud. "It says, 'Meditation and temporary retreat from the outside world. Look deep within and connect with your intuitive voice. Be open to messages from the universe.'"

"I'm that good!" Leo exclaims while nodding in self-approval. "Wait, let's do one more. This time, ask a question. Let's see if it's right," he says while handing me back the card.

I place it in the stack and reshuffle once more. This time, I ask, *What should I expect for the rest of this evening?* I pull a random card. It's the Wheel of Fortune with a wheel as the center followed by eagles in heaven, a snake, and a Devil-like creature holding the wheel. From what I know, this card can have good or bad meanings. I place the card face down once more.

"Guess the card."

He stares up at the ceiling, thinking for a few moments. "This one. It's a wheel. Indicating the unpredictable given the fact that Angelic-like beings and this weird-looking Devil creature are holding it. Expect the unexpected, for sure."

I hand him the card and look up the meaning online. Of course, he is right yet again.

I read the description out loud. "So, it says that this card 'suggests that factors outside your control are influencing your situation. It is as though the Universe is dishing up whatever it pleases; it's unpredictable and unnerving.'"

"What was your intention or what did you ask?"

"I asked what we should expect for the rest of this evening,"

"Interesting," he says while staring off in the distance.

"I think we should get back to reading," I say as I put the cards back into my bag.

"Good call," he returns to reading from the course reader we were assigned.

9 p.m.

I put my headphones on and try to reread the passage by Woolf. I just can't. My mind is checked out for the day. I reach for my phone and notice the time. We've been doing homework for about four hours now and I am exhausted.

"It's time to head back," I say while putting my phone in my pocket.

Leo nods and we begin packing our things and head outside. We're immediately treated with the cool autumn air as well as the darkness of a new moon. Luckily, we have dim lamp posts that line the walkway to guide us back to the dorms. As we walk along the sidewalk, I feel something… squishy. It doesn't feel right. I definitely stepped on something.

"Hold on," I say as I pull out my phone and turn the flash on to check my shoe. *I hope I didn't step in dog poop.*

"Oh, my God!" I scream and step back, dropping my phone in the process, hearing it bounce a few times on the pavement.

"What is it?" Leo takes out his phone and flashes his light on it. "Oh, my," he says while covering his mouth.

A squirrel lays sprawled out, fresh blood oozing from its carcass. It looked deformed, as if it were smashed. "I never thought the death of any animal would look this… *hideous.*" I try to wipe my shoes off on the pavement. That's when it dawned on me. "Dude."

"Yeah."

"I pulled the Death card,"

Leo remained in shock for a second, his eyes wide while he stares off in the distance, appearing to be in a contemplative state. "Remember you also pulled the Wheel one and the Cups one. It told you about unpredictable events out of your control and messages from the universe. Consider this one immense sign of something…"

We both look at each other, then at the body, now aware of the stench. "Leo."

"Yeah."

"I think… I think you're—"

"Clairvoyant."

10 p.m.

After a terrifying encounter with a smashed squirrel and finding out Leo's magical power, I just want to lay down on my bed. I miss it so much: the feel of my fluffy comforter, the soothing caress of my blanket. Just feeling myself sink into the mattress. It all sounds like a serene dream. But that dream is a long walk up three flights of stairs and guarded by the demon that is my roommate, Madison. We used the be best friends, but somehow her privileged family changed her completely.

Now she thinks she owns the entire dorm building. It's horrible knowing that I might have to meet with the RA after I come back to my dorm because I just want to sleep, yet

Madison thinks her now supposed boyfriend has a right to live with us too. I hate my living situation so much.

She always has to "borrow the room" every night of the week and sometimes all day on the weekends. We met with the RA twice to end this mess, but it only got worse. Her whole attitude has gotten worse too. She constantly starts arguments, stays up way too late talking to her new boyfriend every day.

> "Right, baby. I'll make sure to wear that sexy outfit for the party at Triangle... Oh, yeah, you're going to love it," Maddy says in the bathroom, her voice echoing loudly, filling the entire dorm with her conversation. She turns on the blow dryer, it's roaring pitch deafening. All I want to do is sleep for tomorrow's 8 a.m. class. I sigh and throw the covers off me.

> "That's it." I walk over the bathroom door and pound on it. She doesn't respond. I pound as hard as I can and yell, "Madison!"

> She turns off the blow dryer and opens the door. "What?"

> "It's fucking 3 a.m., I have an 8 a.m. tomorrow and I need to sleep."

> "Shit, no need to yell. I thought we were friends, Cur."

> "We used to be." I shake my head.

> "Well, I need top—"

"No," I say while walking over to my bed. She closes the bathroom door and resumes her blow drying.

I sigh and grab my headphones, hoping to block out the noise.

I hate this entire situation, yet I have nowhere to go. I am stuck, completely stuck. It reminds me of that tarot card with the man blindfolded surrounded by swords, known as the Height of Swords. From what I remember, it represents feeling trapped by forces beyond your control, yet if you're able to change your mindset, you can somehow break free from its binds. If only I knew how to break free. Maybe that liberation comes from yelling at Madison and kicking her boyfriend out from the dorm tonight.

Perfect.

I put my keycard in the slot and the door opens with a click. I close the door and immediately feel the chill. Goosebumps cover my entire body, and I begin to shiver. The weather today was shorts and tank top appropriate, but this isn't right. It's like walking into a freezer. I wrap my arms around my body and slowly walk toward my desk, noticing a sliver of light underneath the bathroom door.

I wonder what Maddy's doing.

Suddenly, I hear a faint whisper coming from the bathroom.

I put my ear close to the door. Even though the vent fan is on, I can hear Madison's voice saying incoherent words. "... *If you are here, Lucius, give me a sign…*"

What the hell? What is she doing? Who's Lucius?

I feel my stomach drop to the floor, my body feeling weaker by the second. I manage to walk over to my bed, throw my backpack on the floor, and cover my body with a blanket in hopes of warming up. The energy in the room feels draining and tense.

Maybe it's something I ate?

Something is off for sure. And it's not right.

Immediately, my emotions overwhelm me. Chaos, fear, sadness, and anger. I don't know what to feel. My thoughts begin to race faster and faster, making it incomprehensible to even think, so many voices whispering incoherently in the back of my mind.

I cover my ears with my hands, hoping the thoughts will stop. My body begins to tense up, my heart beating faster and faster, my breathing quickening. I feel like I am suffocating.

I think I am having a panic attack.

I manage to get out of bed, taking my phone with me, and walk toward the door. Before I reach it, I hear Maddy speak again. Despite how I feel, I can't help but hear what she is saying. I try to be as quiet as possible.

I place my ear close to the bathroom door and continue listening. "...*May the leader of the... shadows... me power... will do your bidding...*"

Bidding? Shadows?

What is she talking about? Or worse. *Who* is she talking to? This does *not* feel right at all. Suddenly, I hear… *chanting.*

Madison keeps saying something in Latin over and over but it's all incoherent.

No.

I reach into my pocket and pull out my phone. I start texting Leo, hoping to calm myself down when suddenly, he messages me first.

```
I got a bad feeling. Come over and stay
tonight. Just trust me.
```

Although his suitemate's couch may not be the most appealing bed, I would rather be there than in here. I don't feel safe at all. I'll listen to Leo, especially after what happened with the tarot cards.

I walk over to my dresser, pick out some clothes, and stuff them into my backpack. I head toward the door, placing my hand on the handle, and turn on the light out of fear.

Suddenly, I hear a crack. I look around the room, my eyes setting upon the window. A large crack spans the glass. More cracks soon spread. I am frozen in fear. The window completely shatters, the shards of glass covering my dresser as a cool breeze brushes my hair behind me.

My body is frozen in place, I can't seem to get my limbs to cooperate with my mind to move.

Suddenly, two bright red dots begin to glow, the outline of a black figure appearing on the window frame. I place my glasses back up the bridge of my nose. The red dots turn into cat-like eyes.

Then I hear a... bird.

Caw caw.

A crow.

Now I am *definitely* leaving.

11 p.m.

I run up the hill, feeling the straps of my backpack dig into my shoulders as I carry my clothes, laptop, and books up to Leo's dorm.

"Leo. Oh, my God, Leo," I say in between breaths once the cellphone ringing stops.

"You okay?" he asks.

"You... you are not going to believe what happened!" I exclaim while approaching the front door of his building.

OCTOBER 10TH, 2018
7 a.m.

"You're up," the stage manager tells me as I grip my glitter-covered microphone, its yellow sparkles reflecting underneath the faint lighting. My chest tightens, making it hard to breath. I have to do this. The strumming of the electric guitar grows louder in conjunction with the fast beat of the drums increasing by the second. It's time. The platform begins to lift, the cloud of smoke dissipating as I reach the top, greeting a loud, cheering audience of thousands.

I yell into the microphone, singing my heart out. "Feeling my way through the darkness... they say I'm caught up in a dream... well, that's fine by me..." The strobe lights flash as I run across the stage, ready to sing near the guitarist up front.

The guitarist's gaze is hidden behind his long blond locks. The beats of the music begin to build, the crescendo of guitars, drumbeats, and electronic bass exciting the crowd who are all too eager to hear the drop, known as the pause before the chorus.

Here it comes.

I approach the guitarist, his gaze meeting mine. My stomach drops to the floor.

His eyes are bright red. Suddenly, his smile turns into a large grin that spans from his mouth up to his ears, his hair turning black within seconds. I no longer hear the *screaming of the audience. I turn toward them. There are no more people.*

It was a crowd of dark shadow-like figures mixed with grotesque demonic creatures, black blood oozing from their jaws. I try backing away, but my body is frozen. Suddenly, I hear a faint whisper close to my ear, it's voice deep and raspy.

"So wake me up."

"Shit!" I open my eyes, my breathing quickening. I look around the room, hoping to God I'm not in that demonic hell hole. I see a white stucco ceiling, brown curtains covering the rectangular window. I rise up to my knees, realizing that I'm at Leo's place, which explains the soreness in my neck and shoulders.

I shake my head and rub my eyes, my breathing starting to calm down. I reach over the couch to my backpack and pull out my phone and see the white digital letters saying 7:10 a.m. I still have three hours until my first class. Today is my hell day with multiple classes back to back from 10 a.m. until 5 p.m.

I hate this.

10:15 a.m., Moore Hall

After a horrendous nightmare that I can't seem to get off my mind, I manage to make it to my World Religions class. I try not to remember it at all, but I keep seeing those red eyes staring right back at me when I close my eyes. Those very red eyes are what I saw yesterday during Maddy's seance or whatever she was doing. All I know is that it's not good at all.

I sit down in the front row, hoping that my mind will be forced to focus on the material instead of dosing off.

"Alright, class, let's begin," Professor J's loud voice projects through the speakers. I pull out my laptop, placing it on the lecture desk, pulling up the Google Doc of notes.

"Today we'll be concluding our discussion of Christianity, that last of the Abrahamic religions, and will begin discussing the lesser known religions."

I wonder what the lesser known ones are.

"To conclude our discussion of Christianity, I wanted to discuss why the trinity is integral to the faith as these three may seem like polytheism but in fact are not as…"

So far, the lecture is boring as hell. Professor J continues lecturing about Christianity, which I am very familiar with. This is all just regurgitation of info to me but not everyone else, I suppose.

I could really care less writing this down. If twelve years of private catholic school didn't teach me this, then I might as well deem myself as a non-believer. It's the same spiel of info that's been ingrained in my mind over and over again, like a mantra… a forced, annoying mantra.

I begin to doodle on my notebook, starting with light scribbles, and attempt to shade it in to look like a plant of some kind. Anything to keep me occupied for the next hour and a half. Yet somehow, images from last night and the nightmare keep coming up.

Ow. I feel a sudden painful sting underneath my right arm. I sigh and turn my arm over. *What the…?*

Six small vertical scratches catch my eye, all of them red and puffy. *They are definitely new ones.*

Maybe it was the bush I almost completely fell into this morning? Wait, there are no bushes on my walk. Right?

I start trying to remember my walk here, but my tired mind just won't do it.

The professor's voice brings me back to reality.

"Class, take a five-minute break and brace yourselves for the next interesting religion we'll be covering," Professor J exclaims as he takes a sip of his coffee and shuffles through sheets of paper, presumably his lecture notes.

I look up and notice the PowerPoint is no longer showcasing a large painting of Jesus. Instead, there's a bright purple pentagram surrounded by black flames, the word *Wicca* written across in bright white font.

This is going to be fun.

Everyone starts to chat.

The entire lecture hall erupts into a cacophonous chaos of drama, sports, and Greek life. I hear a guy talking to some chick a few seats down from me.

"Did you hear what happened at Theta yesterday? One of the frat guys jumped from the patio into the pool…"

Yeah. Fraternity guys are just… no. I don't even want to know what happened.

I start doodling on my notebook again but this time I try to recall how to draw a pentagram. I learned this from Maddy last year when she showed me her summoning spell while we sat in a circular pentagram.

I draw a few lopsided stars, and I just fail completely.

"Hey." Someone sitting next behind me taps on my shoulder.

I turn toward the voice, seeing a young woman with dark hair with neon pink streaks, black lipstick that stands out against her white skin, and dark purple eyeshadow.

"This is how you draw it," she says while demonstrating on her notebook, using a purple crystal-shaped pen to do so.

"Oh." I watch her hand move across the page. "I knew there was a certain way to do it. I remember doing it for a class project but then I totally forgot."

"Yeah, you get used to it once you've been a Wiccan your whole life," she exclaims while finishing her pentagram.

"Wow. That sounds so cool!" I reply. "So, you're a witch, right?"

"Technically, yes. But it's important to know that not all witches are Wiccan."

"Really?" I ask while staring at the chair next to her for brief moment.

"Yep. It's a little confusing but I'm sure will learn about it in lecture." She twirls a strand of her purple hair, making a makeshift curl.

"I think that makes sense. I know my roommate identifies as a witch, but she never mentioned being Wiccan."

"Oh, yeah," she explains. "Being Wiccan means you follow the laws of karma and the rules of the Wiccan Rede, both of which pretty much say do no harm or it'll come back and bite you in the ass."

"That's pretty cool! I sort of had an idea about Wicca but I honestly think most of it wasn't true off the internet, you know?"

"Yeah, there's only so much you learn that's accurate. A lot of people tend to stigmatize Wicca so there are many biased sources." She rolls her eyes. "But if you want to learn more than what this lecture will cover, I can teach you."

Holy shit. I found a cool friend.

"That would be amazing! I am so interested in all of these other religions and spiritualities. I've been leaning toward leaving my religion ever since I heard about the Bible talking about women being submissive to their husbands—"

"Yeah, I'm sorry if I offend you," she cuts me off briefly. "But fuck that shit."

"Same!" I reply enthusiastically.

As I was about to continue our conversation, Professor J begins to dim the lights, leaving the PowerPoint with the purple pentagram to lighten the room.

"Now, we're officially done with the Abrahamic religions course. We will now begin the earth-based or nature-based religions that do not follow traditional religions."

He clicks on the next slide, which is black with white letters written in some mystical-looking font, with elaborate curves on the letters. It's like a professional calligraphy. "Let us begin with Wicca."

"Witchcraft, also known as Wicca, is an earth-based religion with Celtic roots that dates back to antiquity…"

The girl behind me whispers, "That's also badass as fuck."

I chuckle as I continue writing notes about the history of Wicca.

The lecture continues, discussing the emergence of modern-day witchcraft, when the professor finally talks about the symbolism of the pentagram.

"Can someone tell me what the points of the pentagram represent?" he asks as we all sit in momentary silence.

"Yes, you in the back, in the red shirt."

So much for knowing your students in a two-hundred-person lecture.

I turn around, facing the girl, who stands up, her red shirt bugging my eyes with the neon blue letters *ATX*. She throws her straight blond hair over her shoulder.

"That pentagram is the sign of Satan and should not be shown to anyone because all who see will burn in hell just like the Satanists they are. This goes against the will of God—"

Oh, shit.

"This bitch," mutters the girl behind me. "Professor." She stands up and projects her voice. "As a Wiccan myself, I can tell you that we're not Satanists whatsoever. We believe in a higher power. We also believe in the power of nature and the stars and revere these natural forces. We don't follow an organized religion like the Abrahamic religions because we believe the ultimate power is actually within us. And yes, there is such a thing as black magic, but most Wiccans do not cause harm to anyone due to the concept of what we know as karma."

She looks straight at the red-shirt chick. "And we Wiccans did not cause catastrophic wars like the crusades or even ones today that fight over the concept of God. You are all hypocrites; saying 'you can believe in my God cool, but if you don't then bam, you're dead.' So in a way, that ultimate God of yours," she says with air quote, "may actually be the leading cause of war and death but hey, you love that God so much."

HOLY WHOA.

She turns around and faces the professor. "Now, in terms of the pentagram, the five points symbolize the four natural elements and the spirit within us. So it's earth, fire, water, air, and spirit."

The entire lecture hall goes silent after she sits down back in her seat.

I am in shock; my eyes widen.

I meet her gaze and whisper, "That's so badass!"

"Thanks," she says as the professor awkwardly starts lecturing again.

"And in case the Christians kill me, my name is Morgana Silverblood. You will be my witness to this battle," she whispers then flips through her notebook, chuckling as the professor continues lecturing.

CHAPTER 3

OCTOBER 12TH, 2018

I finally get back to my dorm, carrying everything from the night before. Living this way is hell, and I know it too. I ended up staying at Leo's place these past few nights.

I should consider moving out, even though it'll be hard, considering it's the third week of the quarter. Madison used to be my best friend and the best roommate ever.

Until she went back home this summer and came back a total bitch.

Once I open the door, I see a large wooden panel covering what used to be the window where that freaky crow thing showed up. I still can't shake that and that nightmare I had. Luckily, there's no Madison.

Thank God.

I place my backpack next to my desk and unpack my clothes, books, and laptop. I walk over to my closet, placing the clothes in the hamper, and walk over to my bed where I collapse with a sigh.

"My God, I missed my bed," I say to myself while relaxing.

Suddenly, I hear a loud ping noise coming from my phone. I reach over from my bed and check my phone, finding an email notification for a class assignment that I already did.

I shake my head and place my phone on my desk. As I lay back down, I catch a glimpse of a black box on Maddy's desk. Normally, I wouldn't snoop through her stuff but at this point, I'd rather be safe than sorry, considering what she did the other day.

I walk over and get a closer look at the box. "What the…?" I say as I read the bright orange letters spelling *Ouija* on the box.

Oh, this isn't good.

I've heard nothing but bad stories about using this. Even though I am all for my New Age things like tarot cards and crystals, this is something I would not ever play with. I really want to get rid of this. I feel goosebumps cover my arms as a sudden cool breeze brushes my skin.

I walk backward from the board until I feel my desk behind me. I reach for my phone, ready to text Leo, when I hear the click of the front door. I am immediately filled with dread.

"Hey," Madison says as she places her backpack on her chair. She glances at me as I look at the thermostat that tells me the AC isn't on.

"Hey," I say as I turn around.

"Oh, Cur. I'm pretty sure you noticed the window."

I turn around, meeting her gaze, quickly glancing at the window then back to her. "Yeah, I was wondering what happened. I've never seen these windows completely break like that."

"I know, right!?" she exclaims. "It's so unusual. I was just here studying with Harden two nights ago and it suddenly just cracked," she says, clearly trying to explain why we have a wooden panel covering it now.

"Harden?" I ask

"Oh, right. He's that Tinder date from the start of quarter. We're dating now though."

"Oh, cool," I say as I look down at the carpet floor. "Oh, Maddy," I say as she starts scrolling on her phone.

She looks up. "Yeah, Cur?"

"Why do you have a Ouija board? You know those make me feel so uncomfortable, right?"

"Really, Cur? It's just a Halloween toy. I bought it for the Halloween party at Kappa Chi. It's not going to do anything scary," she says with a grin.

"Look, Madison," I say, gritting my teeth in frustration at this whole living arrangement. "I don't know what you're doing but it's not good. You've told me before that only experienced witches can use that for some ceremonial purpose and now you're just going to use it for fun?"

"It's fine to play with occasionally, like on Halloween. That's the perfect time to use it."

"Look, Maddy. I don't know what you're doing but I know it's not right. Every time I walk in here, it gets insanely cold and I know that AC isn't on," I say while quickly pointing at the thermostat. "I don't even feel comfortable sleeping in here given the heavy, negative energy that you bring in here!"

"Me?"

"Yes, you. I know what really happened with that window! You were chanting some shit in the bathroom and the freaking crow thing broke that thing to pieces."

Maddy chuckles and shakes her head. "He was right."

"Who? What are you talking about?"

"Someone you'll never know," she says while walking over to the boarded window, gliding her fingertips over the board. "Someone who will help me discover my ultimate potential."

I place my phone in my pocket, ready to leave. *This doesn't feel right at all.*

"You know, Cur. Remember I told you that witches were known as these evil creatures that people persecuted for thousands of years? That it's a myth witches are evil?"

"Yeah." I step away from my desk and walk toward the door. My breathing quickens, my body tenses.

She turns around with a grin on her face. "It's not a myth."

"Okay, Maddy, I'm just gonna…" I walk toward the door and hear a click. I try opening the door, pushing down hard on the handle, but it doesn't budge.

Why the hell isn't this shit opening?

"Curanda, Curanda," Maddy says as I turn around, meeting her gaze. Her eyes are no longer light blue. They're bright red.

She slowly walks toward me. I can feel my heart beating faster, hear the pounding in my ears. I try opening the bathroom door. Nothing. I try opening the closet doors. Nothing.

The temperature drops so low I can see my breath. I pull out my phone, ready to call dispatch, when suddenly it flies out of my hands toward Maddy.

She picks it up and shakes her head. "Really? You think they'd help against a witch?"

I'm out of options. I turn around and start banging on the front door. "Help!" I scream. "Help!" It's getting harder to breath now with the cold air filling my lungs. I try screaming again but can't go on. I start coughing as I turn around and lean against the door, giving up on calling for help. I meet Maddy's gaze, wheezing as I try to breathe. "Maddy... why?"

"You don't understand, Cur. I can become the most powerful witch of all by joining the darkness." She's about five feet away from me now, her red-eyed gaze making my heartbeat faster. "I should've done this a long time ago." The lights turn off, leaving the only source of light her bright red eyes. Suddenly, more bright red, cat-like eyes start surrounding her, followed by growling and snarling.

Fuck.

Suddenly, I see a light coming from my desk, a faint orange glow. The eyes turn toward it, their shadowy form illuminated in the light. The light starts glowing brighter, its orange glow turning as bright as a white LED light. My candle.

My wrist begins to warm, and I look down at my crystal bracelet, noticing it glowing bright white. We are both beacons of light in the darkness.

The red-eyed creatures hiss and begin to disappear, the set of eyes fading one by one. The cold air warms as I lean my back against the door. I catch my breath as the lights in both the bathroom and ceiling turn back on. This time, the room is completely empty. Maddy is nowhere in sight. My phone lays in the spot where Maddy was.

Is this a nightmare?

I reach for the door handle and push down, hearing the click of the door opening. I reach for my closet door, feeling it slide open. I do the same to the bathroom door, which also opens. I sigh and run my hands over my face, briefly shaking my head to clear my mind. I walk over to my desk and notice my black candle.

The entire glass candle is covered in black soot, and the inside has no black wax at all. But what scares me the most is the red object at the bottom. A small bright red fang. I pull back out of fear, making note to not touch that candle ever. I reach for my left wrist where my bracelet is and feel nothing but my skin. I double check my wrist and notice no bracelet whatsoever. I bend down to pick up my phone and turn it on.

I see a text from Leo.

I'm on my way. He had sent it just a few minutes ago so he should be here any minute.

Suddenly, I hear knocking on my door and place my phone in my pocket.

"It's Ally, your RA!" the high-pitched voice exclaims.

Shit. I totally forgot I screamed and pounded on the door. Let's see what I can come up with.

I open the door and see Ally, adjusting her glasses as she glances from the clipboard up to me. Behind her is Leo, approaching from the stairwell.

"Hey, Ally."

"Hey, Cur. Just came by to see if everything's alright. I heard you pounding on the door and raising your voice earlier. I just wanted to remind you that it's disruptive at midnight."

"Oh, right. I'm so sorry about that. And I am fine. Just got into another fight with Madison."

"I notice you two have been having a lot of issues lately."

I sigh. "Yeah. I'm sure you know she's turned into a nightmare roommate."

"Yes. I've been trying to get housing to see if there's any way you can move out, given the number of issues but admin doesn't want to proceed. It's a mess, I know."

"It's okay. Don't worry about it."

"Well, that's all I had to tell you." Suddenly, another guy exits the elevator, wearing a dark police-like uniform, the sound of a radio beeping filling the hallway. Leo takes a step back, allowing the guy to walk toward Ally and me.

"Oh, Max," she says while checking her clipboard then back to him. "I didn't get the heads up that someone called dispatch." I glance at Max. Tall, blond, with black square-framed glasses.

"Yeah, It might've been the dorm room next to hers," he says while gazing at Ally. "What concerned me was that the caller mentioned the yelling sounded like a cry for help, so I had to come up and assess the situation before determining whether UCPD needed to be called."

"Oh, my. I just heard loud noises but not that. And normally, Justin would let me know when dispatch was arriving."

"It's fine, Ally." His gaze meets mine. "Your name is?"

"Curanda, but you can call me Cur."

"Okay, Cur," he says. "I just need to ask a few routine questions to make sure everything's okay, then I'll let you on your way."

Suddenly, Ally's radio goes off. She reaches for it and it emits sounds of an incoherent voice.

"Oh, Max. You'll have to do this without me. I have to do something else in Fir really quick," Ally says as she fumbles with her clipboard.

"Yeah, that's fine," Max says as his gaze moves from hers to mine. "Okay, Cur. First off, are you okay now?"

I nod. "Yeah, I'm fine."

"Do you know what started the yelling?" he asks.

"I got into a really bad fight with my roommate and she stormed out of the dorm. I don't know where she went."

He nods then glances at the window behind me. "What happened to your window?"

Oh, shit.

"My roommate somehow broke it," I say.

"How?"

"I have no idea. I'm hardly ever here since she's always bringing her boyfriend over."

"What do you mean by hardly here?"

"I literally sleep over at a friend's dorm multiple times a week. That's how bad it's gotten."

"Oh, wow," he says then glances back up at the window. "Do you mind if I take a look at the window?"

"Sure," I say while opening the door, allowing him to walk in. I place the door stopper under the door. He walks over to the wooden panel as I lean against the hallway wall, texting Leo to wait in the lounge until Max leaves.

"Um, Cur?"

I look up from the floor, meeting his gaze. "Yeah."

"Did you write these symbols?"

"Symbols?" I ask and walk over the window. He steps back, revealing the panel. My chest tightens. Five black inverted pentagrams stretch across the panel. My eyes widen and I take a step back. "I—I didn't do that."

"Is that your candle?" he asks while my racing thoughts reach a halt. I turn around and see him by my desk.

"Yeah, those are mine. I know those are against the housing rules. I'll put it away—"

"Don't," he says while meeting my gaze. I freeze for a moment as he walks toward the candle and peers into it. Wait. The fang.

"That red thing is part of a Halloween prop. Here just let me—"

"Cur, don't," he says while stepping away from the candle. He looks around the room, his gaze moving from the candle to Maddy's side of the room.

"Do you mind if we talk in private?" he asks.

"Uh, yeah," I reply and walk toward the door, removing the door stopper. I walk back and sit on my bed. "You can sit on my desk chair."

"Oh, thanks," he says while carefully pulling my chair away from the desk, turning it to face me.

"I will say this straight up concerning the symbols and that candle. I know this is going to sound strange and you may not believe it at all, but there's…" He looks at the window then back to me. "There's evil in this room. My guess is that it's obviously not you but your roommate who's doing something that's not okay."

I nod. "I know she's doing something that isn't right. She has a Ouija board and chants weird things. I don't know why—"

"Chants what?"

I shrug my shoulders. "It might've been Latin. I have no idea. I couldn't understand it."

He nods, then sighs. "I don't remember asking you but what's your roommate's name?"

"Madison Scar."

His eyes widen. "Scar as in S-C-A-R?"

"Yeah." I nod.

He looks down at the floor for a moment, lost in thought. "This isn't good at all."

"What?"

"I know who Madison is. You're not going to believe this at all but… Madison Scar comes from a long line of witches who embrace the darkness."

"I know," I reply. "I just didn't know about the darkness part. Before, I would've never thought she'd have any darkness within her but now I think that's changed."

He nods as his gaze meets mine. "I know you mentioned earlier that you were screaming at Madison in some argument and then she walked out of the dorm."

"Right," I reply.

"What really happened, Cur?" he asks.

I tell him a short version of what happened and how the candle ended up the way it is with that red fang showing up out of nowhere.

"Shit," he mutters while shaking his head and sighing. "I'm going to have to tell The Community about this."

"The Community?" I ask.

His gaze meets mine. "You have abilities, right?"

"Why would you think I do?"

"Well, considering that you know who Madison is, what she is capable of, and the fact that you appear somewhat calm talking about all of this. Normally, if people don't have any abilities, they would go insane having witnessed what you did earlier."

Yep, that makes sense.

I nod. "I do. But it's not that interesting though."

"What can you do?" he asks.

"I can resurrect plants." I turn toward my desk, noticing my mini cactus completely brown and shriveled in its pot. "It was alive earlier today, but I guess after what went down, it ended up dying."

"Are you okay showing me what you got?" he asks.

I nod. I close my eyes, placing my right hand in front of me near my face, concentrating all my power on the plant, feeling a rush of energy and euphoria, tingling from my head down to my toes, my body pulsing with energy.

"Wow," he whispers, and I slowly open my eyes and see the cactus rising, turning back to its vibrant light green. I put my hand down as it comes to stop. I turn to him, noticing his eyes widen. His gaze moves from the cactus to mine.

"You got some interesting powers that have a lot of potential," he says.

"Really?" I ask.

He nods. "I can help you find this true potential. I know I mentioned The Community earlier. You've never heard of it, right?"

I shake my head. "Is it a type of frat?"

He shakes his head, chuckling. "The Community is a group of people who have a variety of abilities like you and Madison, minus the evil intentions, of course. They're witches, warlocks, necromancers—"

"Necromancers?" I interject.

He nods. "There are people your age who can resurrect the dead, similar to what you did with this plant except with people."

I look at the plant then back to him. "Do you think I'm one or—?"

He shakes his head. "I'm not too sure but I can figure out who you can meet. Has anything else happened that's been off?"

I nod. "I've been getting random scratches and I have no idea why. I thought I kept bumping into trees along the way, but UCLA doesn't have a lot of trees or bushes. That's why I have a protective candle on my desk and a black tourmaline bracelet, both of which did protect me tonight."

"That will only protect you temporarily now, Curanda." He looks at the candle on my desk then back to me. "With everything's that's been going on, I highly advise that you leave this dorm ASAP. It's not safe to stay here at all."

"I don't know if housing would be okay with me moving into my friend's dorm though."

"I don't think you're safe anywhere on the Hill. So as long as there is no protective barrier that would stop her, there's no telling what she can do wherever you go."

"Well, where am I supposed to go?" I ask.

"I have a room in my apartment complex that you can stay in. No need to worry about rent either. I'll explain it all in more detail later. I know you just met me and it seems weird but you have to trust me," he says while I am just registering the seriousness of this situation.

"How soon should I move out?" I ask.

"Ideally tonight," he says.

"I have no idea how I'm going to move out all of my things by tonight—"

"I have plenty of people who can help out. There's no need to worry about that."

"But how do I stop my housing thing? Like the boring paperwork stuff?" I ask.

"Don't worry about it," he says. "I'll take care of it. I'll get you a move-out cart and everything." He glances at his watch. "It's almost one, so we'll have to move as quietly as possible. Also do you have friends who have powers similar or more powerful than yours?"

I nod. "One of my best friends may be clairvoyant and I know another who is a witch. I think one of them is here waiting in the study lounge," I say, remembering Leo.

"Okay, can you get them to help you move out? I can also provide them with a safe place to stay given the fact that Madison can attack anyone who's close to you."

I reach for my phone and text Leo, telling him to come in to be briefed on everything. I text Morgana as well, not expecting an immediate reply, and begin to pack up my things. Max opens the door, letting Leo in, and tells him about everything that's been going on while I continue packing my things.

Looks like I am moving out tonight.

1:30 a.m.

"Need help with that?" Leo asks as I grab my gym bag, filling it with all the closet things from towels to a bag that's also my makeshift hamper.

"Not with this but you can help with packing my desk things into the container over there," I reply while pointing to the box near my bed. He walks over and starts putting my notebooks into the container.

Meanwhile, Max has gone somewhere as I no longer hear his voice in the hallway. I don't know where he went but I continue to pack. Finally, I hear a knock on the door.

"Cur?" I hear Morgana's voice and immediately walk over, opening the door.

"Hey! I didn't think you'd show up since it's almost two in the morning," I say.

"I knew something was off and as soon as I read your message, I came down." She looks around the room where the boxes cover the floor followed by my suitcase.

"Which one do you need help packing?" she asks.

I lower my voice. "Can you help with packing my clothes in the suitcase? I'd rather not make Leo uncomfortable grabbing my bras and stuff."

"Right," she replies and walks over to my dresser where my suitcase lay open on the floor.

"Where's Max?" Leo asks.

I shrug. "He went somewhere. He was talking to someone on the phone earlier, but he'll be back soon," I say while throwing my gym bag on my bed.

"Max?" Morgana asks while turning around to meet my gaze.

"Yeah, he's the guy I mentioned in the message who's helping me find a place to move out."

"Oh, right," Morgana says while zipping up the suitcase.

"Curanda, can you unplug the wire from your desk lamp? I don't want to drop the candle up there," Leo asks as I'm mid-reach for another bag.

"Yeah. I'll handle it right now," I reply. "Girl, can you hand me the bag of toiletries? They're already in a bag on the bathroom floor but I gotta add them to this other bag." *Packing is horrendous.*

"Sure thing." She walks over to the bathroom and returns, handing me the bag that I pack in a larger one and walk over to my desk, crawling underneath to remove the lamp plug from the socket.

"Girl, quick question," Morgana asks.

"Yeah?" I pull it out carefully to not drop the candle up top.

"Is he cute?"

I immediately pull the wire out of the socket too hard and my lamp falls with a *thump*.

"Oh, shit," I say as the candle jerks side to side. Luckily, it doesn't fall. "Morgana, really? You want me to check out this guy while trying to move out all of my crap? That's the last thing I'd be thinking about right now! And I almost knocked down that stupid candle."

"What's wrong with your candle? Can't you just throw it out? It looks burnt out already?"

I shake my head. "Take a look inside it. Do not pick it up or move it. I am just gonna leave it there. Max says he can help get rid of it."

"Oh, let me see." She walks over and peers into it. "Holy shit!" she exclaims while slowly walking away from it, her eyes wide with shock. "How the fuck did that get there?"

"I'll tell you all about it later, but I'll just say it's the crow incident times one hundred."

Finally, Max returns. This time, he has a large move-out cart, which is what we need desperately, as well as two more people.

"You must be…?" Max asks, looking at Morgana.

"Morgana. The witch friend," she replies.

"Right," he says. "I am sure Cur told you about the move out, right?"

Morgana nods.

"Well, I can tell you more about what I can offer later, but right now, we have to move her out. Also, these are my friends, Will and Avi." He gestures to the two guys behind him. "They'll be helping us with the stuff and they have their cars out in the back lot so we'll be able to move everything to the apartment tonight."

I look at Will and Avi. Of course, I briefly check them out. The tall one has blond hair and blue eyes. I swear he looks like something that came out of EDC. Tie-dye shirt, gray shorts, and he's wearing some type of weird pendant of a neon green skull. He looks pretty cool. The other has dark hair and glasses. I am guessing this is Will. He looks like a nerd, calm and calculated. I feel like I have seen Will before though.

"Okay, Avi and Will." Max gestures to my printer, microwave, and fridge stacked on top of each other. "Grab the heavier items and load them up." They immediately come in, pushing the cart in to load it.

"And Morgana..." Max says. "Can I talk to you outside briefly?" He gestures toward the hallway.

"Sure," she says while glancing quickly at me then walking out with Max.

Now I get to know these two new guys better. Of course, I just wish I had better things to say, given that they're moving all my stuff out. Yet, I want to have a decent conversation. I turn around to my bed, grabbing my gym bag and suitcase, Leo grabs another. As we turn around, I can't believe what we see.

The fridge, microwave, and printer are *floating*.

Both guys are staring intently at the stack, with their hands in the air as if they are holding it with an invisible rope. This looks like something straight out of *Star Wars* when they use the Force. I am in shock as I see the floating mass land with a slight *thud* in the cart.

Holy shit.

"How the hell?" This is the only thing I could muster in my state of shock.

"No worries, newbie," says the guy in the tie dye shirt. "You might be able to learn some spell stuff, but it'll take some time. I am Avi, by the way, and this," he says while gesturing to the nerdy guy who's fixing his glasses, "is Will."

Will waves his hand briefly then grabs the printer, placing it on the bottom of the cart.

"Also, don't say anything to Max about what you saw. We were supposed to do it manually, but we don't have time for it," he says with a smile. He looks behind him. "Don't tell him we're using magic to do this either." He lifts all of my bags from my bed and places them in the cart.

"I am not responsible for any of this. You're getting garden duty next time," says Will.

Avi rolls his eyes. "If the boss finds out I am using magic, he'll just yell at me again, giving me the whole rundown of the Council or some shit. I already know what to expect." He looks at us. "Keep this secret so I can save myself a lecture."

We nod and I notice I still have my gym bag on my shoulder. I look out toward the hallway and back at Avi. "Can you?"

Avi nods. "Place it on the floor. I'll take care of it." He lifts my stuff onto the cart, which is already filled to the max.

"What's left?" he asks.

"Just some closet stuff, the pillows here and the toiletries."

"Good." He nods while looking around the dorm. "Man, I don't know how y'all do it."

"Do what?"

"Stay in this small ass space." He looks at the bathroom door then to Madison's side of the room.

"We manage somehow," I reply. "I am hoping for a slightly bigger space though."

"Oh, you'll get a total upgrade. Trust," he says while walking over to Madison's side of the room, looking at all her stuff on her desk and posters covering the area above it. "I don't want to be mean or anything but is your roommate like the preppy bitch?" He gestured toward her desk covered in pink leopard pattern, perfume, and *Louis Vuitton* galore.

I nod. "Yeah. She's an actual bitch now. I don't know what happened." I stare at the remnants of my side of the room. It looked like the first time I moved into this place, empty and barren. But I am thankful it's this way now.

"We should get this cart down to my car. I'll take it and Will should be up soon with the other cart," Avi says while pushing the cart out the dorm toward the elevators.

Finally, Morgana and Max return. "Where is everyone else?" Max asks.

"Will and Avi went to unload the first cart," I reply.

"Good. I have one more cart here in the hallway to pack the rest of your things," Max says while walking over to my bed and picking up my body pillow. Now we have to pack the huge, blue foam bedding topper. That's what's going to take up most of the cart space. I take off the fitted sheet and begin rolling up the foam sheet, failing miserably. It's like an extremely thick yoga mat except it won't ever fold up. Max reaches from behind me, trying to help out.

His hand touches mine briefly.

Yet it felt like forever; like a surge of electricity, but without the pain. It's almost pleasurable.

What kind of feeling is this?

Finally, we manage to roll it up and the two of us lift the foam sheet into the cart. *I so wish we could use that magic that Avi did earlier.*

"Alright. I will take this cart down. You don't need anymore, right?" asks Max.

I look around, noticing only my backpack and pink suitcase are left. "No. I can carry these with me."

"Perfect," he says while pushing the cart out of the dorm.

That's when I notice how built his arms are.

Not now, Cur.

Now, it's just Morgana and I waiting to load the remaining bags into the next cart. I grab my backpack and carry it, waiting for Will to come back up.

"I need a break," Morgana says, leaning against the wall.

"Same," I reply while leaning against it next to her.

"You know, this Max guy is going to save our asses. You, me, and Leo are going to move asap. We can't be staying here knowing that we have to suppress ourselves. I wanna be able to be a witch the way I'm supposed to be. Not cramped up in a dorm with another person who is *highly* Christian and sees my things as Satanic," she says while staring at the ceiling.

"Did he mention the money stuff or any logistics? He gave me a brief summary but I'm gonna ask for more details. That's what's worrying me the most," Leo says, fixated on the candle.

"Same," Morgana replied. "It's probably a whole lot of complicated but I'm sure we'll be fine money-wise. And I will help out if you really need it. Also…" She looks out toward the hallway, making sure no one is around, then whispers to me, "I low-key think that Max likes you, Cur."

Deep inside, I am giggling like crazy, but, of course, I don't show it.

"Oh, my God, Morgana." I roll my eyes. "Really? Not now."

"Hey, I'm only trying to help," she says with a shrug. "And this Max guy is legit. I'll be moving my stuff out sometime this weekend, and he told me that we're gonna be able to share a room together!"

"What? No way!" I exclaim.

She nods. "He told me it's like a double apartment or something. There were way too many details, and I might've gotten lost at some point of the convo. Either way, we'll be living together."

A double apartment? Morgana can sometimes be so confusing.

"Well, that's cool. We get to live together." I smile, looking down at the floor for a moment.

Finally, Will returns. "Did you two check everything one more time?"

"Nope, but we'll do it now. Just took a brief break," I reply as we start checking under the bed, opening drawers again, checking the closet one more time and even checking the bathroom.

Everything is gone.

"We're all good," I say while picking up my backpack, feeling my laptop weigh me down.

"I can help with your suitcase," Morgana says while picking up the handle.

"I can come along and help you unpack," Leo says.

"Okay. Great. Y'all follow me. The cars are out back and they're already loaded with your stuff, so now all we need is everyone to head back to the apartment," Will says as we walk out toward the elevators.

I decide to zone out while Morgana and Will start talking about school, getting to know each other. I could've sworn I'd seen Will before but I am definitely not in the mood to socialize given how late it is. I know Morgana is a night owl, but I did not expect her to be this social at 2 a.m. And I can tell Leo is tired by the look in his eyes and his yawning that's getting contagious.

Will ends up bringing me back to reality. "Curanda, how bad was it in there?" he asks when we reach the elevator, the doors opening with a *click*.

"It was horrible," I reply. "I feel bad for whoever her new roommate will be. I'm hoping nobody has to though."

We approach the parking lot and amongst the mass of cars, one of them stands out.

A bright blue Tesla SUV.

That's a beautiful car.

Max turns around to Morgana and me. "Our car is the most, let's just say, creative one." We keep walking, getting closer to the Tesla.

This isn't our—

Will reaches in his pocket as we get closer. Suddenly, the doors open upward like wings, followed by the trunk, the pile of bags greeting our eyes.

I look at Morgana, meeting her wide eyes then back at the Tesla.

HOLY SHIT.

Will glances at me then back to the trunk. "You might have to hold your backpack and suitcase in your lap cause we're full to the top," Will says as the trunk slowly closes. "Y'all can get in now to help Cur unpack when we get there." Will walks around the car toward the driver's side.

I lift the last bag in and walk toward the back seat, carrying my backpack while Morgana loads the suitcase. I look up at the doors, admiring the fact that this is my very first time in my dream car. I could never afford this. I just have to ask… How in the world did someone our age get this?

We get in, Leo sitting in between Morgana and me. I swear it feels like a spaceship. Everything is just so comfortable and futuristic-looking. The trunk closes with a click and Max gets in the passenger seat, immersed in his phone.

"Avi is back at the place, right?" Max asks.

"Yeah, he has most of the lighter stuff but the fridge should be fine here," Will replies.

"Oh, can you guys close the doors?" Max asks. We buckle up, realizing we have no idea how to close the doors. They're the fancy wing doors that open upward.

"Uh, how do we?" I ask and look toward Morgana for some knowledge. I feel so embarrassed. I am pretty sure my cheeks are bright red.

"Oh, you guys have never been in one before, huh?" he asks, turning around in his seat, his phone still illuminating brightly with messages.

We both shake our heads. "We've only admired from afar. We both ain't rich enough for this," Morgana replies while I am still in shock. Meanwhile, Leo is fixated on the large dashboard tablet.

"Yeah, my parents would never get me a car like this. Leave it to Will to find a way to snag this beauty," Max replies.

"His parents bought him this?!" exclaims Morgana.

Max shakes his head. "You're not gonna believe it but Will has helped out celebrities. I'll let him tell the rest." He turns around as his phone starts ringing. He starts talking to someone about making sure some meeting gets set up for tomorrow night.

Hmm. Wonder what's happening.

Finally, Will returns and looks at us. "I got the doors. No worry," he says while closing his door. The winged doors close with a click and we start backing out of the spot. Max hangs up his phone just as we start leaving the parking lot.

Morgana and I are quiet until Max decides to let Will tell the story of the car.

"So, Will. They're interested in knowing how you got this. You should tell them how," he says while glancing back at us.

"Right," Will says, adjusting his glasses. "First things first, do you two know what a numerologist is or what they do?"

"Nope," Morgana replies.

"Okay. So in addition to my wizard side, I am able to give people insight on their lives by looking at important numbers in their life from birth dates to dates of passed loved ones or even analyze the figures of businesspeople like CEOs at companies to ensure their business will flourish. Now, I don't like to promote myself, given the fact we gifted people have to be extremely careful about our true nature."

He continues, "So, I consult with them in private. Anyways, word got around and the CEO of a company met with me. After analyzing every important known number in their life, I told them they would be extremely successful. But there's so much more to it than that. After a few months, they contacted me and were wondering where to send a gift of appreciation. So, I let them know my address and when I came home from my internship last summer, my parents were taking pictures of the car in the driveway."

"I am surprised your parents didn't keep it," says Morgana.

"Well, I was gonna give it to my mom, but my name was on all the car paperwork and it would've been a hassle to change it. I let my parents use it for a week until I was able to sell my dad's hand-me-down SUV. They ultimately decided it was best to let it be my car. But yeah, my parents thought I was drug dealing or something," he says with a laugh.

"So, wait." *Now I gotta ask.* "Are you clairvoyant?"

"Not really," he replies. "I can connect with the spiritual realm when I analyze those numbers. I can't just predict what they'll be doing spontaneously like a clairvoyant can. They are capable of seeing into the future on command, which is something I can't do. It's complicated and I'll let Max explain the witch and wizard stuff once we get there in about three minutes."

I feel my eyes starting to close while looking out the window. I just want to sleep. Just leave everything unpacked, make my bed, and knock out. That would be so nice.

As I look out the window, I notice we're pulling into a driveway of a large apartment complex. We start going downward into a garage. Will reaches for a clicker on the window shade and the gates start to slide open. There aren't as many cars as I expected. Maybe around ten or so, but this garage is fairly large. There are at least four or five floors but I am not too sure.

Will pulls into a spot, then opens the back doors and trunk.

"We're here," says Will as everyone unfastens their seat belts, preparing to carry everything. We don't have a moving cart.

Oh, no.

"Everyone just grab what you can carry. We're gonna have to make multiple trips but we do have an elevator," instructs Max as we all head to the trunk to grab a bag. Everyone gets something relatively heavy while I'm left with the pillows and bedding.

We walk across the parking lot, the vast concrete area making everything echo. We reach the elevators and immediately I notice a keypad next to it. Max places one of my bags down and types something into the keypad, then presses the button. The elevator open with a click and we load up inside except for Will, who drops off two bags then heads back to the car.

Once we're all inside, Max presses the button for the third floor. The doors shut, and we ride up to the third floor. Once the doors open, we grab our bags. We are greeted with a long hallway with doors flanking either side.

"Follow me," instructs Max as we walk down the hall. I look at all the numbers, taking in the moment that my new life starts. We turn right and Max reaches into his pocket, pulling out a single key. We reach room 333 and he inserts the key and opens it with a *click*. "Apartment 333 will be yours and Morgana's once we move her in," he says while walking in and turning the lights on.

This. Place. Is. AMAZING.

It has one big living area with our beds, a couch, a small table in front of the couch, and a little nightstand followed by a mini dining room table and, of course, two desks. There's also a cute kitchenette.

"So y'all know what all this is. The bathroom is near the front here," says Max as he walks toward the front the door and opens another door. "You two have this sort of small closet but I tried to maximize the space as much as I could," he says while turning on the lights for the kitchen.

There's no way I can afford this.

"Holy shit! This is our place?" exclaims Morgana as we place bags on the desk and couch. I place the pillows and bedding right beside one of the beds.

"Yep. I currently only have one copy of the key on me, but I will give you a key when we move you in," Max says while meeting Morgana's wide-eyed gaze.

"This is pretty nice and cozy," Leo says while scanning the room, his gaze landing on the window. "Yeah, Leo, your apartment will be a two-bedroom instead and you might have two other roommates, but it'll be larger than this." Max places a bag near the bed.

"That's great," Leo replies while placing another bag on the floor.

"Wait." I grab my blanket from a bag. "Do you own the building or something or are you the manager of this place?"

"My parents technically own this place but I am managing it right now. It's a little complicated but I'll explain more details later. We have plenty of rooms available but the catch is that you have to be gifted. This is a safe sanctuary pretty much for anyone who has the skills and wants to expand on them. So we have a couple apartments that are like this or if you guys want your own studios separately. I'd have to make adjustments, but this is the one I was able to get the fastest. I just renovated this room, anticipating someone might need it. Perfect timing though."

"My God, this is way too nice," I say looking around. "I don't... I don't know what to say. I am at a loss for words at such an amazing place to live in." I take another look around, feeling beyond thankful and at peace.

"I can't wait to live here!" I exclaim, meeting Morgana's gaze

"Same, girl. This is luxury compared to the dorms," Morgana says as she walks toward the bathroom.

"Cur!" She calls me over. I walk to the bathroom and notice a big grin on her face. "It has a tub! I can finally get bath bombs." Morgana is an absolute Lush fan, especially with their bath bombs.

"I can finally try a legit Lush bath bomb," I say with excitement.

"Alrighty, girls," Max calls from the living area. "Let's finish unloading everything. I will talk to you, Cur, about everything in the morning."

We walk out of the bathroom and head out of the apartment, repeating the process of bringing things from the car. This time, Will is with us as we unload the rest of the stuff. Now all I have to do was unpack, which I am so gonna leave off for tomorrow as I feel so damn exhausted.

"Alright. That's everything from the car," says Will as he adjusts his glasses once more.

"And Avi has your microwave and printer. He'll bring those up but do you want the mini fridge? Otherwise we can put it in storage," Max tells me while answering yet another text message from someone.

"If you can store the fridge, that'll be nice. I just need the printer in case," I say while unpacking all my bedding. I gotta lay down now.

"Okay. Well, this is everything. Do you need us to help you unpack?" Max asks while gesturing to everyone.

I shake my head. "I'll be fine. I am just gonna load the bedding and toiletries. I could use some sleep now," I say, hoping everyone would leave.

"Perfect," says Max. "Will, can you take Morgana and Leo back to De Neve? I'm sure we can all use some sleep."

"Sure," Will says as I check my phone for the time. *2:30 a.m.*

"You can follow me." Will leaves the apartment, Morgana and Leo following.

"Bye, Cur!" Morgana and Leo say while walking out.

"Bye!" I finally put the fitted sheet on my bed. I throw a couple pillows on there as well. It's been a long night.

OCTOBER 13TH, 2018

I throw off my blanket, stretch, then head to the kitchen. I had expected to have absolutely nothing in the fridge but see a gallon of milk, almond milk, and a carton of eggs. I close the fridge and check the cabinets above the fridge. There's a plastic bowl and some organic chocolate cereal. *Okay. Who knew that I love vegan chocolate cereal? That's weird.*

I grab the bowl and the box of cereal and set them on the counter. After the cereal's all gone, I start opening the bags of things on the floor, unpacking everything one by one. It seems like forever, but I organize my desk and fold and put away all my clothes.

As I'm putting away the last of my clothes, I notice my favorite outfit of all: my bright blue polka dot jumpsuit. I haven't worn it in a while, but I seriously crave the comfort of it. Might as well look stylish unpacking, right? I walk over to the bathroom, moving my toiletry bags away from the doorway and close the door. *Wait. There's no one here.* I'm just so used to doing this.

Once it's on, I admire the way it fits, trying to see all of it through the counter mirror, but I also notice a body mirror behind me on the door. I turn around and see the entirety of the outfit, the semi-loose pant legs making the romper appear flowy, the bright blue contrasting with my dark skin, accentuating my curves I've always been self-conscious of. It looks beautiful yet it's so comfortable. I also get a close look in the mirror, noticing the dark circles that have become more prominent lately due to the whole sleeping at Leo's place and last night. I feel for the hair tie in my bun and let my hair loose, admiring the feel of it against my neck. I've never really have time to look at myself this way but moving here has allowed me to feel comfortable doing so.

Plus, this moment of self-love and happiness motivates me to keep on unpacking so that I don't have to step over my bags to get in here. I walk over to my backpack sitting by my desk and unpack my laptop and my velvet bag carrying my small altar, which is pretty much a candle, a star-shaped obsidian crystal, a pack of incense cones, and a dreamcatcher that I usually put by my bed. I manage to make some space in the right corner of my desk right next to my lamp.

I admire the fact that this tiny altar always makes me laugh due to the size but also how this managed to survive the whole Maddy incident last night. I do want to have a larger one like the ones I've seen on Pinterest with large elaborate crystals, tons of candles, and statues of deities. Those are altar goals.

Suddenly, I hear knocking. I walk over to the door, noticing that there's a peephole and look through it, seeing Max's blond hair. I flip the lock and open the door.

"Hey, Max," I say.

"Hey, Cur. Just wanted to check in to see how unpacking has been going," Max replies.

"Yeah. I'm almost done. I've been unpacking since nine this morning," I say with a sigh.

"Wow. That's almost like three hours!" he exclaims.

"Wait, really?" I pull out my phone, checking the time. It's ten till noon. "Oh, my. I didn't think it'd take that long."

"Yeah, I should've stopped by earlier to help. But I am here to let you know all the details about logistics with the apartment and The Community. It's gonna take a little while but do you have time right now?"

"Oh, yeah, of course." I open the door wider. "Come on in." I step aside, allowing him in.

"Alrighty." Max checks his phone and puts it away.

"I'm gonna explain everything so you don't have to keep worrying about logistical things." He closes the door and grabs a chair from the dining area. I sit at the edge of my bed. I'm a little bit nervous considering that it's just the two of us in a room alone. But I know he doesn't have bad intentions. I can sense it.

"So, you run this entire place?" I ask.

"Technically... yes." He runs his hand through his hair. "I run this entire building because my parents are involved in this council known as The Council of Mystical Beings. They are like a governing body over those who have powers. They provide us with protection, ensure the legitimacy of our gifts, and have some rules to keep it hidden from people who aren't gifted. We just call them mortals for short. So my parents are part of The Council and I run a chapter here at UCLA that allows us gifted folks to have a safe haven to practice our powers while staying hidden from mortals. We call ourselves The Community, and by us I mean this whole entire apartment complex."

I nod, taking everything in. "I never thought that there was an actual governing body that can help us. It seems so strange."

"It's a lot more complicated and I can explain more about The Council later. But for now, I need you to know that I do run this place, and I'm giving you this place to stay for free."

"No way," I say. "I can't, this is so—"

"It's okay. You don't have to pay anything aside from your necessities, but there is a catch."

"What's the catch?" I ask, suspicious now, rethinking everything.

"You have to keep up with weekly meetings. The Community has them once a week to discuss current news of what's going on involving anything magic-related. You must also abide by informal rules, which are that you only practice your powers here in the apartment complex, preferably the Training Room, and try to avoid doing it on campus because we can't be seen by mortals or those without powers. In this day and age, if someone were to get us on camera, it would be a mess to avoid being exposed." He checks his phone briefly.

"Also, as I briefly mentioned yesterday, this entire building has a powerful protective spell on it that ensures no outsiders will be able to see what magic you're doing or how you're doing it. It's kind of like an invisibility cloak. And we have this powerful spell courtesy of The Council. The members of The Council are extremely powerful witches and wizards, so this spell is going to protect us from everything, and mortals won't be able to look in and see what we're doing.

"Also, another catch is that since this entire building is The Community, we have to keep the apartment building tidy. So if there's maintenance we have to do, we can all pitch in at some point but if it's something really major I could try to negotiate. Pretty much like doing chores too but around the building if that makes sense."

"Yeah, I get you," I reply.

"Cool. But yeah, this will be your living space for your time here at UCLA or even if you decide you wanna live in Westwood, you are more than welcome to stay. Although most people end up moving away after college. It's up to you though. I think that's most of what I needed to tell you." He checks his phone once more.

Wow. I am at a loss for words, and I can't believe that this just happened. I feel so... I don't even know how to explain it. It's like an insane miracle.

"This is just so amazing. I can't believe it. I have to repay you somehow," I say.

"Don't worry about it. Money shouldn't be an issue for your protection and guidance as well. Given that you have this unique power, I'm going to have Avi be your mentor. You met him, right?" he asks.

I nod. "He's the one with the tie dye clothes, right?"

He gives a slight laugh. "Avi is an interesting guy. Loves to party and even DJs but it's mostly EDM stuff. Anyways, as part of being in The Community, I pair everyone up with a mentor. Someone who may have similar powers who will teach you how to manage them or even discover more. Based on what you showed me, I think Avi will be your mentor for now. It seems like you may have necromancer skills."

"Necromancer?" I ask. "What's that?"

"Well, it's someone who is capable of bringing living things back from the dead. And by living things, I mean humans, plants, pretty much anything living."

What? I can bring people back? That just sounds pretty morbid.

"So y'all can meet at anytime. It's up to y'all to meet at least once a week though. I will make sure to check in on you two at some point in the week as it is essential to enhance your powers. This mentorship is also part of the agreement. In terms of practicing your powers, there's a Training Room in the basement. You remember the garage we parked in, right?"

I nod.

"Well, there's a floor below that's about the size of that garage that's dedicated to practicing your powers, reading about anything magic-related, and of course, a room for the necromancers. We keep it closed off for obvious reasons but one of the main things is that sometimes Avi might bring in a dead body and will attempt to try and figure out what happened to it. He really doesn't do that often though but just in case, we have a separate area for that. He'll show you everything once you two decide to meet." He checks his phone again. "Is there anything else that you have question-wise for me?"

"Well, this isn't related to what you said but how come you keep checking your phone? Just can't help but notice," I say.

"Oh, I keep checking messages in the group chat. I have to be on top of everything that goes on within The Community. Let me add you so you can be notified about meetings and everything."

"Of course." I get up from the bed, and he hands me his phone. I make sure to check my number and hand it back to him. I don't know what to ask him. I really just want to explore this whole building now.

"Perfect," he says while putting his phone in his pocket. "Any other questions?"

"I don't know what else to ask. You laid out everything pretty well."

"Great. There is one thing I have been meaning to ask. Do you practice voodoo or Santeria or anything similar to it?"

I shake my head, confused. "That's a weird question to ask."

"I know, but I have to make sure there isn't any hardcore animal sacrifices or black magic. That is not tolerated here whatsoever."

"Oh, yeah, no. I don't touch that at all. I don't mess with any of that stuff. I just have some candles but I don't mess with any bad magic."

"Great," he replies. "I know you must be tired from all the unpacking but if you're up for it, I will be having The Community meeting right now at around 1 p.m. You can come if you'd like but I won't make it mandatory for you since you just moved in."

"Of course, I would love to learn more about all of this!" I exclaim.

"Alrighty. So follow me." He leads the way out of the apartment, locks the door, and hands me the key.

"So, we're going to head down to the second floor, which is the communal area. We have our meetings there and it's pretty chill. It's very different from the magical practicing area. You'll find out when we get there," he says while we wait for the elevator. "Wait, it's one floor down. Let's take the stairs." He opens the door next to the elevator with a large red exit sign placed on it.

We reach the door labeled with a 2, and right away we're greeted to a large lounge. It has about four couches, a row of fold-up chairs, a large whiteboard in the front and wooden podium. Everything minus the podium resembles a dorm lounge like the one back in De Neve. All of the seats are occupied with about 20 unfamiliar faces either gazing down at their phones or facing the people next to them talking. I notice Will talking to someone else while Avi, wearing a bright neon orange shirt and a tie dye bandana, relaxes on one of the couches with his hands behind his head.

I take a seat on the far left next to a girl who's looking up at the podium, her bright purple dress contrasting with the red floral pattern. I cross my leg away from the chick next to me, shaking my foot nervously and hoping my flip fop doesn't fall off. Suddenly, I feel a tap on my right shoulder. I look toward the girl sitting next to me, her brown eyes meeting my gaze.

"Hey. You must be the new girl right?" She pushes the feathered clip in her hair away from her eyes.

"Yeah. I'm Cur and—wait. How'd you know? Did Max already tell everyone?" I ask.

She shakes her head. "I can sense new energies and auras immediately. You have a strong, positive vibe and a bright blue aura."

"Wait, really?"

She nods. "I can share more with you later,"

"That would be awesome!" I exclaim.

"Oh, I'm Akasha, by the way. Also…" She looks over her shoulder then back to me. "You're gonna need a friend to help you navigate the social sphere here. There are some peeps here who have cliques. Very few though, but I'll help you avoid a few petty arguments. You see the group in the back?"

I turn around and see a group of three people. Two guys and a girl in the middle, all wearing fancy clothes similar to what Madison wore.

"So the girl in the red dress with the platinum-blonde hair is Sabrina. She's one of the witches who sees herself as better than everyone. She's an entitled brat who thinks she owns The Community."

"Really," I asked

She nods. "And to top it off, she's always had her eye on Max. I honestly think she's trying to get with him but I'm not exactly sure."

"All right Community members," Max says, interrupting us as he takes the podium. "We will begin our meeting in a different way today as we are welcoming a new member to our building and we will be having two other members joining in the next few weeks as well. Curanda, why don't you introduce yourself?" He glances at me then back to the rest of the folks sitting.

I stand up, intimidated by all the eyes staring at me. Of course, I notice Avi with his neon T-shirt though. I can't believe he's my mentor. We're definitely going to get along if he loves EDM because I love that music so much.

"Hi, everyone. I'm Curanda. Y'all can call me Cur. I can bring some things back from the dead, and I don't know what else to say, but yeah." I wave at everyone then sit back down, noticing how hot my cheeks feel from embarrassment. These folks can probably do way better things than I can but oh well, I have to admit my gift.

"Welcome, Curanda." Max glances down at the podium. "So, to begin this meeting, I just want to hear about anything else new in general. Let's start with Will. Is there anything that I should be concerned about immediately?"

I turn back to Will, who looks up from his whispered conversation. "Well, aside from the frat dudes getting too high off of acid and weed and throwing a party across the street, then seeing a guy streaking, I don't think we have any imminent threats."

"Great," replies Max. "Does anyone else have any announcements or anything before I start talking about what The Council needs me to say?"

Everyone shakes their heads and the room is silent for a moment.

"Alright. So let me pull the message from The Council." He pulls out his phone and scrolls for a second.

"So, The Council wants me to inform you all that they will be visiting within the next two months. I don't have a specific date yet but when I do I will let y'all know. For any new members who don't know what happens when these visitations occur, we have to be on our best behavior. That means don't be casting spells on people just to mess with them, and make sure to clean your apartment living areas as well as keeping up with chores. Also make sure that the Training Room is cleaned as well. Make sure that once you're done practicing your magic in there that you cleanse the area before you leave. Courtesy sage and palo santo are provided, although Maria has told me that it is bad for the environment. We're trying to find other ways to smudge the area, so I am going to look into that. But I'll explain more as the day comes.

"I do have some reminders: Make sure that you guys are practicing only in that area but if you do it in your room, I'm not gonna be able to see it. Just make sure it's nothing too drastic that people outside will see. Like if you're doing divination and you cast an animal or something in your living area and it can clearly be seen out the window, try not to do that."

Akasha chuckles next to me. I can't even imagine what conjuring up an animal would look like

"Also, if you notice any crimes that might've involved magic, please inform me right away so that I can formally report it to The Council, and we can figure things out." He glances at everyone once more, and the people down the row to my right, and some others are nodding.

"Yeah, I think everyone is up to speed on things." Max drums his hands on the podium. "Also make sure you all sign in with the app before you head out and make sure you are meeting with your mentors at least once a week. That's the bare minimum so that you can learn how to enhance your craft and so you're not causing explosions in the Training Room. With that, I guess, I will dismiss. You're all free to head back to your rooms and enjoy the rest of the evening or for casting spells at midnight. Good luck to you all."

Everyone starts walking toward the exit, creating a small crowd. Suddenly, Max calls, "Also, if any of you have questions for me, I live on the first floor in room 111 so feel free to knock at any time, although I do like my sleep but if you have anything urgent, feel free to come down."

I nod and as I wait for the crowd to lessen, I feel a tap on my shoulder.

It's Avi. "Hey, so if you want to meet sometime tomorrow, I can show you our special room for necromancers that's downstairs in the basement. I can meet you right by the elevators on the third floor. Oh, and I can give you the printer then."

"Yeah, that's fine. I just can't wait to do this, you know," I say while waiting in line.

"Of course. It's exciting when you're first practicing or you're discovering more about yourself you never knew about before. Plus, it's been a while since I've been a mentor. Not too many necromancers, you know. You should enjoy this time right now."

"I definitely will," I say while walking out behind the crowd.

"You're added to the group chat, right?" Avi asks.

I nod while signing in.

"Perfect. I'll message you on there. Later, Cur."

"Bye, Avi," I say as we all head of down the hall toward the elevators.

CHAPTER 4

OCTOBER 14TH, 2018

I hear a buzzing noise. It's so annoying. I am just enjoying my time, relaxing in a pool, feeling the desert heat and sunshine warm my skin. I so wish I could do this forever.

Wait, that buzzing noise.

Get up, Cur.

I wake up and pinpoint the buzzing noise coming from my phone. I reach over to the nightstand and look at my phone.

I have texts from Avi, Leo, and Morgana. First is Avi.

```
Let's meet at 11. By the elevators.
```

I glance at the time. It's 10:30 a.m.

Oh, shit.

I throw off my blanket, stretch, and then head to the kitchen. I prepare some cereal and settle down on the dining table, checking my phone's alarms. I somehow slept through multiple ones. I check my other text messages really quickly I check a text from Leo.

```
I'll be moving in next weekend. I
can grab us dinner once you're all
settled in.
```

Then Morgana:

```
Leo is excited to move in. We're finally
gonna feel safe.
```

Well. At least it wasn't anything too serious from them.

I just can't wait to start practicing. I check the time again. 10:50 a.m.

I gotta go. I grab a comfy gray romper from the drawers beneath my bed and quickly change.

With just my phone and key in hand, I lock my door and head down the hall, awaiting Avi's arrival. As soon as I reach the elevator, the doors open and Avi stands there in another tie-dyed T-shirt. This time, it's a blend of blue and purple shades.

"Oh, perfect timing," he says while holding the doors open.

"Thanks." I walk in, making sure I place my key and phone in my pocket.

He presses the B button and the doors close. "Ready to start practicing?"

"Yeah!" I exclaim. "I want to start but I don't know what 'practicing' actually means."

"Well, I'll just be showing you the Training Room where everyone practices, the Reading Room, and the Necromancer Room just to get familiar with the floor in general. You probably won't do any hardcore spell casting today. It's more like an introduction."

"Oh," I reply, slightly disappointed but excited that I get to see where the magic happens. I feel the elevator jerk to a stop, and Avi opens a compartment on top of the elevator buttons, revealing a keypad.

"I've never seen that before," I say while waiting for the doors to open.

"Yeah, We have to make sure it's secure since it holds a lot of precious things," Avi replies as the click of the buttons fills the space. Suddenly, the doors begin to open. I immediately smell palo santo and white sage, the sweet aroma instantly relaxing me.

"So, here's the Training Room." Avi walks out of the elevator.

I am in awe.

I'm greeted by the sight of this large room lit up with bright white light. Four large black workout mats cover most of the area with black cushions lining both the walls.

"Here is where we practice self-defense spells. Everyone is taught this no matter the power you have," he says while I follow him toward the right corner where a large black cabinet lies with practice dummies lined up next to it. He stops and reaches for the handles.

"Now here is where we keep the practice weapons, some of which only experienced practitioners can use." He opens the doors. A white light automatically turns on, revealing shelves containing wands lined on top of each other, knives hanging from their handles, necklaces with crystals hanging on a jewelry holder, along with crystal bracelets and a large trunk with a lock on the bottom shelf.

He reaches for one of the wands and shows it to me. Right away I notice four different purple and red stones lining vertically along a light brown wood, the tip of it containing a large clear crystal point.

"This one is everyone's favorite," he says while turning the wand over.

"Because of the color, right?" I ask.

"That and what it's capable of doing. It'll pretty much protect you from any offender by freezing them—and not the cold freezing way but more like stopping time kind of way."

"What do you mean by stopping time?" I ask.

"This pretty much turns them into a statue, stuck in their position for a certain amount of time, allowing you to either run or attack them further," he says while turning around and placing it back on the display.

"And those necklaces and bracelets are actually amulets you can wear to protect you outside of The Community from any form of danger, magical or not." He pulls a necklace off the holder and turns toward me, allowing me to see the silver chain and crystal pendant. It looks like a round pink rose quartz with some type of geometric symbol in the middle and a small opal stone in the center.

"This one looks like some type of fancy necklace," I say as Avi holds it in his palm.

"It's actually a protective amulet." He raises it up by the chain and allows the pendant to dangle. "Once you start learning defensive spells, you'll actually be carrying this one with you."

"Wait, what?" I exclaim. "How...?"

Avi nods. "Everyone gets a protective amulet of some form whether it's a bracelet or necklace. So you'll learn how to use this one really soon." He places it back.

"And now the trunk on the bottom is only for advanced practitioners so you can't open it just yet." He closes the cabinet doors. "Now, I'll briefly show you the Reading Room, Apothecary, and the Necromancy Room," He walks over to the other side of the room where three doors are located toward a brown door on the left.

"So, this is our Reading Room, which is pretty much the library here. We'll have to be quiet and you'll be able to explore more after this." He slowly opens the door. The smell of parchment and ink hit me. The lighting is slightly dimmer than the Training Room. The smell of a book is something you can't fully describe but it's the best smell ever.

There are bookshelves lining every single wall filled with books with bindings of different colors and textures. A few books have their bindings sewn with string and the parchment of one appears as if it's slightly cracking. I follow Avi as we walk toward the back, and I notice a few books titled *Potions, Mastering Tarot*. I stop at one book with gold words written against a dark blue binding. *Cunningham's Guide to Wicca*. And another bright purple one titled *Immortality Elixirs*.

In the center of room are rows of desks, some of which have a divider, all of them having lamps and office chairs. Avi gestures toward the door at the far end of the room. I notice some familiar faces from the meeting yesterday flipping through various book pages. We continue walking and suddenly I hear a whisper coming from behind me. I turn and see Akasha waving and mouthing "Hi" with a smile. She approaches us.

Avi turns around and glances toward her. "I didn't see you earlier so I didn't know if you'd be here to give the tour," he says while turning to me.

"Why would she give me the tour?" I ask.

"Oh, I didn't mention it yesterday?" Akasha asks me. I shake my head. "I'm actually the librarian. I should've been down earlier but Avi seems to be doing a good job."

"Yeah, I was going to show her the door to the old texts," Avi exclaims.

"Oh, yes." Akasha walks head of us toward the door. "Here is where older texts are that need special care. You might be using a few at some point so you need to be careful with them. If you ever need to access it, just let me know."

"Thanks," I reply.

"Is that all you two need?" Akasha glances at Avi.

He nods. "I have to show her the Apothecary then the Necromancy Room."

"You mean, the room of the dead," she replies with a chuckle.

"Sure." Avi rolls his eyes.

"Well, you two," Akasha glances at Avi then me, "have fun on the tour. I have some organizing to do in the back." She waves goodbye as we walk toward the entrance we came from. We finally reach the door and slowly step out.

"What do you think of the library?" Avi asks.

"Honestly, it's amazing. I will for sure be there all the time," I say with excitement.

"Wait until you see the Apothecary." He walks over to the green door, knocks twice, then opens it. A bright LED light shows a tall wooden cabinet with shelves of glass jars filled with herbs and powders. On the other side of the room is a display case holding a variety of different colored class candles and baskets containing more pillar candles of different colors, shapes, and sizes.

"So the cabinet here that takes up most of the back wall is filled with herbs and spices used in spell casting. These are mostly just natural herbs while the cabinet on the left over here," he walks over and opens the door, taking out a jar filled with purple and pink herbs and small bits of something shiny, "is where we have prepared spell mixes that were made by a team of witches and magical botanists." He hands me the jar to inspect it. The label is scrawled *Celebrate*.

"I am guessing this one starts a party, right?" I ask.

Avi shakes his head. "It's actually a pick-me-up type of spell. So when you're feeling down, you take a little bit of it and burn it on some charcoal and once you inhale some of the smoke, your mood will improve. It's sort of like an anti-depressant but definitely not a replacement. It's just for temporary use," he says as I hand him the jar.

"You'll also notice that we have two sinks, one here and on the other side. That's because candles and potions have to remain separate or some type of fiery explosion can happen." He walks over to the cabinet of candles. "Now, here you'll be able to do candle magic that can involve creating a candle from scratch or using the plain candles on the shelves to help you. You can use already-made potions and herb mixes to dress the candles, but the candle has to be unlit while dressing it. You know what dressing it means, right?"

I nod. "It's when you add bits of herbs, carve symbols and names, or place oils on it, right?"

"Exactly. You want to make sure the candle is dressed first before lighting it. You'll be able to do so in the other room behind this one." He gestures to a door next to the cabinet of herbs. "That room is like the laboratory that gets messy but can handle fire."

"Wait. So you don't use any fire in here, right?" I ask.

"Right," he replies. "You pretty much use only herbs and unlit candles here and in the back room you light the candles or mix the potions. Think of this room as the supply room and the back room as the laboratory."

"Oh. That makes sense." The colorful candles remind me of *Aura Vita* minus the labels stating their magical intention.

"I'll let you explore more of this later, but I do want you to see the Necromancy Room," he says while walking toward the entrance.

I follow him out and head toward the aluminum door I remember seeing earlier. As we approach the door, I notice a sign that reads *DO NOT ENTER. AUTHORIZED PERSONNEL ONLY* in black letters. Avi places the key in the knob, and the door opens with a creaking noise. I smell chemicals similar to formaldehyde, the scent that I hated when dissecting frogs in high school. It's pitch black until Avi flicks on the light.

This place is not too inviting. It honestly looks like a miniature morgue. There's a large metal table placed in the center and everywhere else around are metal cabinets, white countertops, a large sink, and linoleum floors. It reminds me of that time I visited a coroner's autopsy table for my medical program. And the smell. It reeks of chemicals and antiseptics.

"I'll admit, this is probably one of the scariest places in this building." Avi approaches the metal table, turning around and leaning against it. "We have it like this since we are necromancers, so we do bring things back from the dead. It's not a pretty process either."

I walk around, examining all the metal cabinets and a large fridge in the corner of the room. I do not want to know what's in there.

"I'll show you one of the cabinets that contains only animal specimens." He reaches for another key and opens the cabinet, revealing glass jars of organs. I notice a small brain and another that appears to be a fresh heart next to it. I can't recognize the organ next to it because it just looks like a red blob. I can only imagine what it really is. I immediately start to reconsider enhancing and embracing my gifts because I so do not want to have to dissect things.

"I can assure you those organs are from small animals like rats. For the most part, I do work on roadkill like raccoons, possums, and the occasional cat. But rarely, if ever, a human. There's too much risk in doing so around here," he exclaims while I glance at the gray brain sitting at the bottom of the jar.

"So that's pretty much the tour of the entire floor where all the magic happens," he says while I turn around and meet his gaze.

"All of this is so amazing. It'll take a little more time getting use to this room though."

"Well, you probably won't be here often considering you are a very beginner. You will mostly be working with plants but potentially some animals too. I will help you work your way up to that. I'm just here to give you a quick tour and give you your first assignment for this week. I'll let Akasha know to get you the books you need to do the this work as well as help you learn more about what it means to be a necromancer."

"What kind of assignment will this be?"

"It's very simple. It'll pretty much involve you resurrecting a part of the garden in the back while also taking notes on how you feel during the exercise and observing the change in the plants itself. I'll message you a copy of the assignment in more depth and the page numbers for it so you'll get familiar with it. Oh, and I totally forgot. I need to get you some oil from the Apothecary," he says while I follow him out of the Necromancy room.

He locks the door and walks over to the green door, knocking twice then entering. He walks over to the cabinet on the left and pulls out a large jar of green oil.

"Just curious but why do you knock here? I notice you didn't do it for the library."

"It's because if someone is in the middle of crafting a potion or candle magic that involves chanting, they can't be disturbed." He reaches into a drawer, pulling out a syringe and essential oil capsule.

He takes some of the oil from the large bottle and places it into the capsule. He screws the lid on and shakes it a few times. "Perfect," he says while wiping the bottle off with a towel. He shows me the roller-ball capsule, the yellow-green oil swirling inside.

"The assignment will require you to do a beginner spell that requires you to recite the affirmation it has written in the text then take this little bottle of Jericho oil and rub it on your wrists. I want you to channel energy toward a dead plant in the garden. It can be any plant, but the dead cactus out back could use some work. I've been meaning to bring it back but haven't had the time."

"Wait. What's the purpose of this spell?" I ask.

"This spell is going to help you tune in to your powers and enhance them a little more. It's a little exercise to demonstrate your powers. It'll be simple," he replies.

"Thanks." I place the Jericho Oil in my pocket.

"That'll be all for today because I am sure you want to explore more. And, I totally forgot I can give you the code now to access B-floor."

"B-floor?"

"It's what we call this entire floor," he says while typing in the code. "It's a lot easier than saying 'place where we do magic training.' You get what I mean, right?"

"Yeah, that makes sense," I say as he hands me back my phone.

"And if you need anything, I'm a text away."

"Thanks!"

"Well, I gotta get back to that raccoon that I found yesterday." He glances back at the Necromancy Room.

"Good luck with that," I say as he waves goodbye. I place my phone in my pocket and hear my stomach growling.

Right. I have to buy food. I am my own chef now.

4 p.m.

I arrive at the library noticing it's completely empty. I reach for my phone, ready to message Akasha when I suddenly hear her footsteps.

"Cur!" she exclaims while carrying a few books in her arms and walks over to a nearby shelf, placing the books into slots. "Sorry, I had to organize some last-minute books but I do have yours." She walks over to a nearby desk containing a stack of books. She pulls one from the top of the stack, its binding tied together by brown string.

"This book is *Giger's Book on Necromancy*." She walks over and hands me the book. "Make sure you only read the sections Avi tells you before you get to the other ones. It can be pretty dark if you venture into the book alone."

I examine the cover. I notice a silver skull with a red snake wrapped around it and slithering out of one of the eyes.

"Did Avi tell you which sections to read?" she asks.

I pull out my phone and re-read Avi's message. "Yeah. It's one of the practice exercises in the Botany Resurrection section."

"That'll be an interesting read," she says as I meet her gaze. "Hopefully, you can help us get our garden back."

"What happened to it?"

"Well, our succulents have been dying, and Avi seems to never have time to help them." She rolls her eyes.

"I'll see what I can do about it then." I glance back at the book, turning it around to read the summary.

Suddenly, I hear a ringing noise and Akasha reaches for her pocket, pulling out her phone. I can't seem to hear most of the conversation. It's mostly just "Yes... uh huh..." She finally tells whoever's on the phone that she'll be heading out.

"Hey, Cur, I have to run upstairs to help someone out so I'll be back. Enjoy reading the book and try not to head to the back with all the special books that need care. I'd rather not let them get damaged."

"Oh, yeah, no worries." I sit down at a nearby desk as she walks out. I turn the page to the Resurrection Botany section and notice exercises written in old English with a step-by-step guide followed by a spell that contains words in what looks like Latin followed by a description of it in English.

> *When reciting the spell, keep a distance away to allow the plant of choice to rise. With Jericho Rose oil upon your palms, face them upward and begin reciting the spell*
>
> *Surge profundis a morte vitam*
>
> *This spell allows the plant to rise from the depths of death to life...*

"Well, this is boring," I say out loud. I am curious about what the other spells are though. Although I shouldn't read the other sections, I still want to know what else is in here.

I place my phone at the page of the plant spell, making sure not to lose my place and use my hand to flip through the other pages. That's when I stumble upon a black and white image of the face of a woman with dark lines resembling hair, her eyes shaded with the darkest color I've ever seen and her skin drawn with cracks all over her body, her mouth open, revealing sharp teeth. Goosebumps cover my body just seeing the image alone, but I began reading the text underneath it.

Invoking The Lady of Death.

I should turn away from reading this but it's too tempting to pull away.

Should you choose to invoke her in the taking of a life, prepare the black roses on the floor, the hair and blood of the victim, and recite the words below.

No.

It's a death spell.

I immediately close the book, taking my phone out, and take a few steps away from the desk. My heart begins to race. My entire body tenses up. My gaze fixates on the book out of shock and fear. My mind begins to race. I'm terrified of looking at the spell—hell, even the entire book. I don't feel comfortable doing this at all. We have the power to raise the dead but also kill? I really don't know about this. I don't think this is where I belong.

What necromancer fears death?

Maybe this isn't my true calling.

"Curiosity got the best of you, huh?"

I immediately jump back, feeling the bindings of books against my back as I move backward into a nearby bookshelf. Luckily, I don't feel any books on my head yet. I glance toward the source of the voice and see Max; his gaze moves from the book to me.

"You scared the shit out of me. I—" I'm still trying to get my breathing under control and am at a loss for words.

"That's what happens when you read too far into Giger's book. It's not for the faint of heart." He opens the book, flipping through the pages. "You started training with Avi, right?"

I nod. "I needed to learn a plant resurrection spell to formally channel my powers to heal a plant out back."

"Which plant?" He meets my gaze.

"It's some cactus that Avi told me needed help. I figured I'd help out."

He sighs. "I've been telling him to do it for weeks. He shouldn't be making you do his chores for him."

"I'll admit that the spell thing is a little challenging to understand," I say. "But I think I'll be able to do it."

"Wait," Max says. "Did Avi just expect you to read this spell then go on your own to practice it?"

I nod.

Max sighs again and shakes his head. "I had high hopes of him mentoring you but I guess I'll have to take over for now."

"Are you a necromancer too?" I actually haven't heard what his powers are.

"Oh, no, I'm not, but I do know some info about them." He picks up the book, inspecting the cover. "Avi told me about the importance of this book. It's usually the starting point for every necromancer."

"Yeah, I don't think this is meant for me at all." I walk back to the desk.

"I can sense that might be the case considering your reaction earlier. Giger's book is dark but necromancers are able to handle this."

"Really?" I ask.

He nods. "It's been passed down from a long line of necromancers. Luckily, it's partially translated into English."

"Yeah. I've noticed that there's an English description underneath the spell but I have no idea how to pronounce the spell itself." I pick up my phone, checking the time.

"It's unfortunate the Latin couldn't be translated since the words give the power needed for the spell to work," Max says. "That book came from Avi's family back in Sweden, so the descriptions used to be in Swedish. It would've been impossible to understand both Swedish and Latin."

I sigh and put my phone down on the desk. "I don't know if this whole necromancer thing is meant for me after all. Reading this and seeing the Necromancer Room, which looks like a mini-morgue—that scares the crap out of me."

"Yeah, this may not be your calling," replies Max. "I initially thought that you were one considering the fact that you are able to bring the plant back to life. No one else besides Avi is capable of doing that."

"I'm just hoping I'll find something here that'll help with discovering the true power of what I can do aside from just bringing plants back to life. Maybe those herbs and candles can help me," I say. "Gotta ask but why do we have the whole Apothecary, self-protection amulets, and wands?"

"We all can practice magic and do beginner spells. We all have that ability within us. But we have an overall strength that is unique to us. Like Will. He's able to look at numbers in one's life and determine the divine importance of it. He can actually gaze into the past given those numbers while Akasha can access a hidden library that documents the journey of our soul from its inception to now."

"So, she's clairvoyant?" I ask.

Max shakes his head. "She's able to access a realm that no clairvoyant could ever reach. It contains every single action we have done in our past lives until now. It's not so much divination. She'll be able to tell you a lot more about it because it can get a little complicated."

"That is amazing," I say while scanning the stacks of books nearby. "No wonder she's the librarian here."

"Yeah. This is the perfect fit for her," Max replies. "Anyways, you can see how Will and Akasha have vastly different abilities, both of which I can't do, but we all can learn and practice doing simple banishing spells if we wanted to or can practice defensive magic."

"So what you're telling me is that we all have the ability to practice some magic but we have this one special gift that no one else but you has?"

"Exactly. We can all cast some spells but not all of them. That one greatest gift is a defining feature unique to each of us."

"Got it. So I technically can do spell work but I have one special gift that no one has."

"Mmhmm. That's why I am trying to help you find what that gift is."

"Oh." Realization dawns on me. "I understand now. Totally get it. So I don't know mine yet, but what's your greatest strength or gift thing?"

"Oh, mine bothers some people so I probably shouldn't say."

"Tell me, please. I won't freak out or anything," I say.

"Well." He looks off into the distance, silent for a few moments. "I am able to read and manipulate people's thoughts, emotions, and feelings."

Whoa.

"That's… insane," I say wide-eyed.

"Yeah, I don't like to mention it. It's a powerful gift but I am just thankful it's in good hands."

"Huh." I close the book. "Can you read what I am thinking?"

"Cur, I'd much rather not," he says.

"Come on! I promise I'll keep my mind clean," I say with a laugh.

He grins and shakes his head. "Okay. Let me see what I can do."

"Okay." I look away, so he doesn't feel pressured. I try thinking about the most random thing of all: Pigeons. That'll make for an interesting conversation.

"Hmm." He's quiet for a few moments. "I can't—" Suddenly the door opens and Akasha comes in and walks toward a bookshelf in the back. "Hey." She reaches the bookshelf and begins scanning the rows.

"Someone's in a rush," Max says while glancing at Akasha.

"One of the Lunar Twins ended up casting a silence spell and they need to find out how to reverse it. They always do this." Akasha says.

"Lunar Twins?" I ask Max.

"They're witches in training," he replies. "They should be spell casting down here, but they obviously don't listen. Hence why situations like these always happen."

"A silence spell sounds so cool," I exclaim and glance at Akasha, who keeps looking at different shelves to find the book. "Will I be able to do that?"

"Unfortunately not. That's considered advanced spell work only a witch can handle," he says.

"Still, this whole spell casting magic thing is so cool," I say as Akasha finds the book and walks out.

"Yeah. It's interesting what magic can do," he says.

"How about we get away from death spells and start with basic spell work?" He walks across the room toward a bookshelf where Akasha found her book at. He scans the titles of the books and then pulls one out.

"This book will help you understand the basics," he says while handing it to me.

I look at the cover. It had a large sun and moon on it as well as a pentagram right in the center. It read *Introduction to Witchcraft* by someone named Stan Cunningham.

"Witchcraft?" I ask, confused.

He nodded. "This is the best book to learn about the concept of magic, spell work, and understanding how to survive with this gift of overall spell work. It'll be a light read but necessary for you."

I flip through the pages, quickly scanning them.

"So I normally don't mentor others considering I am so busy, but I want us to meet a few times a week to discuss the things you're reading," he says while I decide to linger on a page that talks about the use of candles during ritual, also known as the time when casting spells.

I nod and close the book, admiring the cover once more. "Yeah, we can do that."

"Perfect. And when the time comes to work with candles and herbs, I'll guide you on what you need from the Apothecary."

"Awesome, " I reply.

"In the meantime, until we meet sometime next week. I will text you as soon as I know when I'm free." He briefly checks his phone then returns his gaze to me. "Read the introduction to magic section and do the basic grounding exercise. I have to go to the fifth floor to check up on the Lunar Twins' chaos."

"Have fun with that," I say with a chuckle.

"Oh, I know I will," he says while walking out of the library.

Meanwhile, I decide to skim to a random page in the book. I stumble upon a list of herbs and ribbon colors. It's instructions for a spell. I flip a page back and find the name of the spell: *Hex Reversal*. I read about the basics of it and decide to walk over to another shelf to discover something else new. I scan the bindings until I stumble upon a row of books titled *Mesoamerica*. I scan the titles of the books and suddenly hear a voice in the back of my mind.

Upper shelf, fourth book from right.

I tiptoe and count four books until I reach one with a yellow binding with two green snakes lining it. I carefully pull it out of its spot. I look down at the cover. It has an Aztec statue with the title: *Curanderismo: An Introduction to Mexican Folk Healing and Magic.*

Curanderismo? I've never heard of that before. I flip to a random page and find a section titled *Types of Curanderos and their Specialties.* And see the first one on the list:

> A Hierbero, an herbalist who can call upon the powers of la luna y sol to grow the herbs necessary to cure illness, reverse curses, and increase longevity, even immortality. Legends say they are descendants of the Aztec god Xipe Totec, who's the god of the harvest. They're capable of growing and saving the harvest through inherent magic that resurrects plants from wilting to new life.

Wait.

This has to be me. This has to be my true power, right?

Looks like I have *a lot* of reading to do.

CHAPTER 5

OCTOBER 18ᵀᴴ, 2018, 7 P.M.

Reading about self-defense magic is pretty interesting but not as great without practice. I am a little nervous about meeting with Max today because I read very little of the book. Although learning about the history of magic from ancient times of alchemy to the Salem witch trials and finally to the modern-day practice known as Neo Magic is interesting. I do need to read and pay more attention to the self-defense spells. These are the main way to ensure that I am protected outside of The Community, especially since Madison is on the loose. I am trying to take notes on them given that today Max and I will be reviewing the concepts so that I can start practicing next week.

He left me with this book for approximately four days, and I already did the grounding and basic exercises, but he decided to extend the reading all the way to the defensive magic section. It's been so hard to focus on anything magical given it's midterm season and I have so much reading for my research class. I barely made it to the self-defense portion of the section.

In terms of the self-defense techniques, the other forms of self-defense magic like setting up a barrier with visualization or chanting incantations to create a protective barrier around an object are also interesting too. But the wands and spells for immediate use are probably the most important ones. I start reading at the top of the page, tracing over the black Pentagram that separates the sections. This one, titled *Wands and Spells for Defense,* finally describes the wands and a few of the spells to use with or without it.

> *The wand should be treated with respect, handled with care while utilizing during self-defense. Never to be used outside of defense. Pairing the wand with the word of defense spells enhances the power and efficiency of the magic. Word alone can be used in times of immediate action. The spells below correspond to the type of defense.*
>
> *Rediro (get back) pushes opponent backward.*
>
> *Glacientar (freeze) momentarily makes opponent immobile.*
>
> *Impetum (shield me) blocks defender from physical and magical attack.*
>
> *Volante(float) allows defender to temporarily levitate up and over opponent.*
>
> *The following are offense spells used to attack...*

I tap my pen against the desk as I read over my scrawled handwriting, trying to understand the main concept and importance of the spells. This should be easy but right now it totally isn't. I look up from my notebook toward the bright yellow *Curanderismo* book. Maybe I can read this to take my mind off of the spells. I flip to the introduction and begin reading.

> *Curanderismo is a Mexican folk magic that involves rituals and practices designed to improve humanity through the utilization of powers bestowed upon those gifted by birth. Curanderos, known as the practitioners of the magic, are said to have been long descendants of Aztec gods and goddesses capable of utilizing the powers of these gods to heal the ill, defend against the darkness, and sustain Pachamama (Mother Earth). There are three main categories that correspond to the actions above: Sanadores (Healers), Guerrors (Warriors), and Salvadores de la tierra (Earth Saviors).*
>
> *Each category contains different types of Curanderos who are said to reflect the powers of a specific god; The Healers embody powers of Toci Tonatzin, the great mother known as the patron goddess of healing, the Warriors embody the powers of Huitziliopochtli, the god of war, and the Earth Saviors embody powers of Tlaltecuhtli, the spirit of the earth. The book is split into three parts; each discussing the practices and rituals used by Curanderos corresponding to the overall category...*

I immediately turn the page and see the table of contents, looking for the section titled *Salvadores de la tierra (Earth Saviors)*. I flip to page 120 to the introduction and history of the Earth Saviors. I begin to read the first line when suddenly, my phone vibrates on my desk. I look up from the book to see a message from Max.

```
I'll be ready in 5. Last-minute meeting.
```

I check the time on my phone. Oh, crap. We should be meeting at 7 p.m. I can't believe that much time passed. Luckily, he is temporarily busy too. I grab both my notebook and both the Witchcraft and Curanderismo books and speed walk toward the elevator.

The doors open and I see Will buried in his phone. "Hey," I say as the elevator doors close.

"Hey, Cur. Which floor?" he asks.

"First floor," I reply.

"I'm guessing you are meeting with Max, huh?" he asks.

I nod. "You live on the first floor?" I never knew which floor he lived on.

"Yeah. It's me, Max, and Avi on the first floor. Avi is my roommate and Max gets his own place," he replies.

"It must be interesting living with Avi, huh? Considering his taste for EDM?" I ask.

He nods. "Being his roommate is tough. If you're the type who wants peace and quiet, you definitely won't get it."

Suddenly, the elevator dings as it stops on the first floor. As soon as the doors open, I can hear faint bass music filling the hallway.

"Well, here we go again." He sighs.

"Oh, Will, where's Max's room?" I ask as we walk out of the elevator.

"It's the first door to your left." He gestures to the apartment with the 111 plaque.

"Thanks." I walk over to Max's and briefly glance at Will heading toward his apartment with the bass music.

I check my phone then knock a couple times.

It's a little nerve-racking, knowing that Max is my mentor. I don't know what it is. I always feel so nervous around him considering he's pretty much the leader of The Community. I also think he's really attractive with his gray eyes, blond hair, and toned arms. I'm pretty sure he's toned everywhere though. Back in the library, I didn't really notice it, considering the book having scared the crap out of me followed by his sudden appearance. But now that we're meeting for an hour, I am definitely gonna notice the effect he has on me. So, I'm a mix of nervous with slight mix of excitement. But mostly nervous considering I didn't get so far reading.

"So you must be new girl? " I glance back and see a girl wearing a red dress with platinum-blond hair.

It's Sabrina.

"Yeah, I am new to The Community,"

She walks over and leans on wall on the other side of Max's door "Yeah, I saw you and Akasha in the front row at the last meeting. Normally, I am in the front row but of course, Max has the meeting last minute and I get a spot in the back."

I nod. There's a silence for a moment then she continues, "So, why are you here to see Max?"

"He's my mentor but he's in a meeting right now so I'm waiting for him."

"Well, that's new. He's never done that before." She puckers her lips and shifts her gaze off in the distance then back to me. "You know Max is like the hottest guy in The Community. I just wonder who he'd end up with," she briefly looks as her nails then back to me. "Don't you see how hot he is? "

This doesn't sound good.

"I don't think I should talk about this with you."

"Come on," she exclaims. "Let's face it, most of the girls here swoon over Max. How can you not? The only issue is that none of them are his type."

She looks me over from head to toe.

What the…?

"Especially you. So as long as you're not blonde and white, you won't ever be his type."

You didn't just say that.

"How about you just fuck off and leave me alone."

"Wow. New girl has an attitude."

"You really are a mean-ass bitch."

"Oh, honey," she begins, but the door opens and I turned around, facing Max.

He glances at Sabrina. "Sabrina. What are you doing here?"

She meets my gaze and smiles. "Just wanted to say hi to the new girl." Her gaze moves toward Max. "I didn't know you're a mentor. That's something new."

"Yeah, I am and I have my last meeting of the day with Cur right now so I'll be busy for the next hour."

"I can still meet with you tomorrow night, right?"

"I'm pretty much busy all week for meetings so if you need to schedule a time, we'll have to discuss this later."

"Okay, cool. I'll text you then."

"Sounds good. Bye, Sabrina."

"Bye," she exclaims and subtly glares at me then walks away.

I really hate her.

"Come on in." He opens the door wider. His apartment is a lot larger than ours, which is expected. There's a large living area, with a couch on the right side of the living room and the TV in the center on top of the stand. The center table has a couple pillar candles decorated with autumn leaves at the base.

I see canvas prints of nature photographs, one of a tropical beach above the couch and the other one of the woods that stands out against the white walls. I also notice a large kitchen off to the left followed by a slight hallway on the right that probably leads to his room and bathroom. The candles are lit, and he has a copy of the book that I'm reading on the table.

"Please, have a seat. You can sit on the couch or I can pull up a chair from the dining room table. I also have beanbags in my room. Up to you."

"Thanks." I nod and decide to take a seat at the other end of the couch. I place my stuff on the center table and reach for my Witchcraft book, pulling out my pencil from the wand section I left off on.

I really don't know what to expect from this mentor meeting but I'm hoping I can learn as much as I can.

He sits down and picks up the book flipping to a random page. "So, how far did you get?"

"I managed to get to the defensive magic section and I believe it's part three, self-defense." I gaze over the underlined phrase of the wand's use.

"Well, you got pretty far considering I only gave it to you about three or four days ago." He flips to that section. He glances over the page, then flips it over, nodding. He looks up at me.

"With that in mind, do you have any questions for me right off the bat?"

"Yes." I nod and stare at my book and start flipping to a page where I knew I *definitely* had a question. But somehow I didn't ask about that specific page. "I get that you're trying to teach me about spell casting basics and magic. But what am I exactly protecting myself from? Is it those demons things I saw back during the Madison incident?"

He nods. "It's pretty much those demon things and their human followers. Those demon creatures are known as The Dark Shadows."

"The Dark Shadows?" I ask.

"They're these evil beings that have been wreaking havoc upon the earth with the ultimate goal of conquering the entire planet."

"Oh, wow. I didn't know anything about this. Where do they come from?" I ask.

"Well, it's a long story. You won't need the book for this." He nods to my book.

I place it on the table and sit back on the couch. "I understand that but like we get this ability. Where do we get it from? I'm so confused about that."

"So, there's this ancient tale that goes back thousands of years. It's a tale that everyone who is gifted or has these abilities is taught if they come from a family that has this." He looks toward his canvas print of the woods. "Thousands of years ago, there were these mystical beings called Light Beings."

I interrupt briefly. "What did they look like? Like, are they Angels or…?"

"That's the thing, we don't know what the original Light Being looked liked. Legend has it they were just orbs of white light, but we can't know for sure since they were here since the dawn of time. We don't know what they were originally called so we just labeled them as Light Beings. That's what has been passed down via oral tradition."

"Interesting," I say while following the story.

"Yeah. It is said these divine beings came from another realm outside of the universe, somewhere in a higher realm that is unattainable for us. There's this entire realm of these beings in this divine place. And so these divine beings had created the earth in its unique form by embracing the four different types of elements, which you know are air, water, fire, and earth.

"These light beings wanted to make another unique changes to this planet as they have the four elements, but they also wanted something else. So they created man. And when they created man, they were intending for man to be perfect beings like these Light Beings since they are the embodiment of love, light, and tranquility. But once they created man, that perfection completely disappeared."

"I'm guessing that didn't go well with the Light Beings, right?" I ask

He nods. "Of course, they were upset, so a few Light Beings gathered up a very small group of humans and bestowed them with their abilities that included the gift of practicing magic and of harnessing energy. And so these gifted beings didn't really understand what their gifts were until they started to realize that they couldn't resonate with the rest of the human world. They realized that they were different. When normal humans, called mortals, saw these beings' powers and what they were capable of, they saw these gifted beings almost like gods and goddesses, as this gift came long before race or gender were established.

"So, for a millennia, these gifted beings were seen as gods and are portrayed that way in many myths and stories due to their different gifts and abilities. Well, there came a time around the fifteenth or sixteenth century when science, mathematics, and all the concept of logic started developing that made people realize these 'gods' aren't actually gods after all. And since they couldn't explain what this ability had come from—"

"They were known as evil?" I say.

"Right. What they were doing was deemed heretical, as the concept of only one God who was unattainable was rampant at the time. So these gifted beings were labeled as heretics, eventually called witches, even Satanists. So everybody with this gift is now ostracized because of this stigma that surrounds it and because modern religions look down upon the idea that our gifts made us gods."

He continued, "Well, along the way there were some gifted ones who wanted to keep that god label. They wanted to be honored and known as gods but not for the purpose of reclaiming their power, but to garner that power over humanity. This is the opposite of what a Light Being stands for as they are the embodiment of peace, love, and tranquility—so everything positive. The beings that wanted that power behind the god label wanted to be worshiped. They didn't want to continue being peace, love, and what have you."

"So, I am guessing that these power-craving beings did anything they could to get that, right?" I ask

"Exactly." He runs his hand through his hair. "They confided in evil, almost demonic-like forces known as the Dark Shadows. They promised immense power that would allow them to be worshiped. And so these very few humans ended up becoming Dark Shadows themselves."

"So, that's what Madison ended up becoming?" I ask.

He nods. "Your whole encounter with her involving the crow, the incantations, and the red fang all hinted at the presence of the Dark Shadows."

"Oh, shit." I briefly remember the encounter with Madison, her red eyes staring back at me, scaring me to the core.

"Yeah. So we are gifted with our unique abilities but we can be tempted to the Dark Shadows. That's why it's important that we not only stay hidden just for our own safety but also to practice correctly and not take advantage of the powers that we have."

"Yeah, that makes sense," I say while briefly staring at the candle.

"I'm surprised you weren't told anything about your powers or your gift. Most people who do have family with powers are informed about it when they're children or when they first discovered it."

"I never knew about any of this until now. I come from a family of hard-core Catholics. I don't know if there is someone in my family who's done this or who has the ability or gift. Even if they did, my parents would make damn sure they didn't get anywhere near me," I say with a laugh.

"Well, what made you delve into the spiritual or new age thing?" he asks.

"I didn't like the fact I was forced to do all the Catholic things like going to mass, doing the sacraments, and all that. It didn't feel… right," I say while meeting his gaze. In this moment, I feel that calm emanating from him, feel his welcoming demeanor. He seems interested in my backstory too.

"Plus, I had been exposed to the concept of magic when a friend showed me *Harry Potter*."

"*Ah*. Everyone has some film or book introduce them to some form of magic," Max says with a laugh.

"Yeah. My parents were not even okay with that in the house. Then when I was around five or six I first discovered my power to bring plants. I wanted it to look green again."

"Why?"

"Why what?"

"What made this plant special when you used your powers?"

"It had been my grandmother's favorite flower. She passed away when I was five, but I can somehow remember her taking care of that plant every time she used to visit us."

I remember the fight my parents had when the plant died. *"Goddamnit, the plant died." I can see my mom, upset after yelling at Dad.*

"It used to bring me happiness. I used to look at it all the time whenever my parents argued."

Max is quiet. Nodding. Understanding. "You don't have to answer but did your parents have issues with work?"

I shake my head. "My dad is an alcoholic. My mom used to get into horrible fights with him and kicked him out a few times. I don't know why I am telling you this," I say as feel the tears coming, my chest slowly beginning to tighten. My mind goes back the memory I'd always hated.

I hear my mom's voice in the back of my head. *"Get the fuck out! Now!"* She's screaming at dad again. Why does she have to do that to him? Why? WHY? It's all overwhelming. I need to get out. I need to run.

I feel tears stream down my face as my perception returns to Max's apartment. I try keeping it together but my sniffles turn into full-on bawling.

"Cur, it's okay, it's okay," he says as I feel his arms wrap around me, letting me cry into his chest. Even though my thoughts are flying a mile a minute in my mind, I feel… *safe* in his arms. I don't know long I've been here but I slowly begin feeling the sadness go away. I nod and Max releases me. I wipe my tears away, sniffing. I no longer feel nervous around him. That feeling just left.

"I am so sorry." I pick up my books. "I should go—"

"No. No, it's fine. You can stay if you want," Max says.

"You probably think I am crazy."

"No. I don't." His eyes lock with mine. Something in the back of my head tells me: *stay*.

I smile and take a seat next to him on the couch. "What else should we talk about?"

"Anything you'd like or that you're comfortable talking about."

I sniffle. "Can we go over the self-defense spells? I barely had time to go over them."

"Of course," he replies. "It's hard to remember them when you're first learning but with practice, you'll get the hang of it."

"Also," I say while pulling out my Curanderismo book. "I think I might have some idea of what my true power may be." I flip over to the page with the *Hierbero* description.

"This sound very similar to what you've told me. I've never seen this book before." Max scans the page. "Did Akasha help you find it?"

I shake my head. "I found it hidden on one of the shelves in the Mesoamerican section."

He nods. "Can I take a look at the introduction?"

"Oh, yeah." I hand him the book. He flips through a couple of pages and stops, reading the text for a few moments.

"Interesting," he says.

"I read the first chapter and it looks like they have a creation story that's similar to the one you told me. I'm guessing it's just a different interpretation of it?" I ask

He nods while flipping the page. "The one I told you is the overarching idea, but other cultures can interpret it in their own ways." He closes the book and writes something down on his notebook. "I'll ask Akasha if we have any other copies of this so that we both can read it. I'd advise reading more about the section you showed me earlier. I am not familiar with this but we definitely can both discuss what we get."

"Perfect," I say as he hands me back the book. "I am also gonna see if there's any outside sources relating to this too."

"Sounds like a plan." Max picks up his copy of the Witchcraft book. "So you had trouble with the self-defense spells?"

OCTOBER 19TH, 2018, 9 A.M.
"So here's the backyard and the garden." Max opens the back door on the first floor. He leads the way in front along a stone walkway lined with succulents on each side. The right side contains the notorious large light cactus and a few mini round succulents and cacti, while the other has a large agave succulent and a round red succulent. All of them starting to, or are already, wilting.

"So, this place pretty much needs a lot of help." He steps aside, allowing me to get a full view of the backyard.

Along the path in the center of the yard is a water fountain about the size of a birdbath, the stagnant water forming a puddle in the bowl. The path continues toward the back with a stone bench in between two rose bushes that are starting to wilt. The grass encompassing the entire backyard is yellow-green and rough from the lack of water. On the left side of the yard is a white shed, its door partially revealing a shovel, and the right contains a large garden box that occupies the entire left side of the yard filled with dried green sprouts of unidentifiable plants.

"What happened here?" I ask while eyeing the garden box.

"We used to have someone who maintained the garden and provided the spices of the Apothecary. Luckily, not a lot of people need the spice for spells but it's only a matter of time before we run out so as long as this garden is like this."

"Can't Avi help bring all of these back?" I ask.

"He can't bring back the entire yard. Plus maintaining the plants is the most important part. We can't just keep resurrecting them left and right," he replies.

I nod. "That's true."

"I wish Shasta didn't have to leave. We could've avoided all this mess."

"I'm guessing Shasta had powers like me, right?" I ask.

He shakes his head. "She just loved gardening. She would help maintain and eventually dry out the herbs needed for the Apothecary. We all know how to do that but it's been so hard trying to find the time."

"That makes sense with everyone trying to balance schoolwork and having to practice their powers while remaining hidden. It's been hard for me to even get through the readings you've given me." I walk over to the garden bed, looking at the wilted sprouts. I crouch down and push one of them aside, seeing a white thread forming a box around the plant with a plastic pick protruding from the ground. The word *Basil* is scrawled along the pick. I look up from the plant and notice a grid formation lining the entire bed, each plant occupying a spot with similar plastic picks placed in the ground.

"Well, I've never been a gardener before but I can definitely try. I'll bring back a majority of the plants and maintain them." I stand up and turn toward Max.

"That would be amazing!" Max exclaims. "It would also help you understand your potential herbalist skill from your book."

"That's why I wanna test it out." Suddenly, a thought came into my mind. "I totally forgot I got a large agave succulent from the market over the weekend. It's actually way too big for my desk, and I'd love to plant it along the path."

"Feel free. It's all yours." He gestures to the entire yard. "The watering can and hose are next to the garden. If you need the gardening gear like gloves and shovels, they should be in the shed." He gestures toward the shed. "I don't remember how to get the fountain working but I'll ask Will. He usually fixes all the tech and structural stuff so don't worry about that."

"Perfect." I follow Max back to the toward the back door.

This will be interesting.

4 p.m.

The smell of wet dirt fills my nostrils as I dig a hole next to the round red succulent, placing my agave in it and patting down the soil around it. I briefly water it and continue resurrecting the other succulents that have yet to be healed. I cup the wilted succulent next to it, feeling the warmth in my hands while channeling energy to it. I begin to feel its form move and I move my hand away as its brown wilted form turns back to its original dark green. I look at the row of succulents that line each side of my agave, all back to their original dark and green colors.

I have the right side of the succulent line done but there's another side to go. I take off my gloves and take out the Post-It with the resurrecting plant spell I wrote down and place it on the dry grass next to me. I aim my hands over a small wilted cactus and recite the spell out loud in Latin as best as I can. *"Surge profundis a morte vitam."*

The cactus returns to its dark green round figure, its top glowing bright pink. The spell worked just as well as my power to help this one, but I do want to try something different because going one at a time takes forever. No wonder

Avi didn't want to help bring them back. I just can't figure out how to do it though.

Suddenly, I hear a voice in the back of my mind, similar to the one back in library.

Water the ground, place your hands upon it, visualize the line of plants, channel.

I grab the watering can and water the entire line of wilted succulents, making sure the soil turns dark. I kneel near two small flower-shaped succulents and place my hand on the ground, visualizing the line of dead succulents. Suddenly, I feel warmth rise from my arms down my body, something totally new. I open my eyes. I am in awe. The entire line of succulents begins to rise, all of them blooming and turning different shades of green. I usually can only do one at a time. This can't be me. I turn my gaze around left and right, trying to see if there's anyone else who might've helped me do this.

There's no one in sight.

I have an idea. I wipe my hands on my pants and reach for my phone in my back pocket, to check the time. I see a message from Morgana sent an hour ago.

```
On my way. Clear the space!
```

That's when I see a notification from the group chat with The Community that Max sent out.

```
If anyone can help us move in the new
members, lmk.
```

Well, I completely forgot.

I leave the gloves and watering can next to the succulents and head up to the third floor to help Morgana out. I enter the stairwell off to the side of the elevator and make my trek up two flights. As soon as I open the door, I see Morgana walking down the hallway with her rolling suitcase toward the opened door of our apartment.

"Girl!" I exclaim while walking toward her, trying to catch my breath.

"Cur!" she yells while running toward me, giving me a huge hug, leaving her suitcase behind. "I am so happy I was able to move all my stuff over this weekend."

"I'm glad you're finally here. It's been a little lonely in the apartment."

"Oh, I'm sure you enjoyed this past week to yourself, huh?" she asks.

I nod. "I kinda did but I'm happy you finally moved in."

"Yeah, moving in is such a hassle." She glances at her suitcase. "I have no idea how you moved your stuff overnight. And you have way more things than I do and here I am struggling."

"Yeah, I don't how I did it either," I say. "But I'll help you unpack because that's the most time-consuming part."

"That'll take all evening, right?" Morgana grabs her suitcase, rolling it toward the apartment.

"Yeah, it might." I walk in as Max and Will place her other bags on the floor near the couch and her bed.

"Hey, guys," I exclaim.

"Hey." Will walks toward the door. "You need help with that, Morgana?" He gestures to her suitcase.

"No, it's fine. Cur will help me unpack this and everything else." She gestures to the side of the room filled with multiple bags and boxes, certainly less than I have.

"Okay, cool." Will glances at Max, placing the last bag on the floor.

Max turns to Morgana. "So, I'll give you a tour of the apartment later tonight or tomorrow. And, Cur?"

"Yeah?" I ask.

"Can you get Morgana set up with the group chat and kinda give her a summary of B-floor? She'll get the in-depth tour of the entire apartment but a little introduction to it can help her and us out."

"Oh, yeah, I can do that. I'll be helping her unpack tonight but we'll let you know how far we get," I say as Morgana rolls her suitcase next to her stuff.

Max glances at Will. "We'll head out then and if you need anything, just message me."

Will says goodbye as I kneel to unpack her first box labeled Desk Stuff.

"Oh, Cur," Max calls to me right before he leaves.

I look up. "Yeah?"

"I'm thinking of adding Saturday or Sunday for our mentorship meetings. Would you be okay with it?"

"That should be fine, yeah," I reply.

"Cool. I text you more about it later." He makes his way out of the apartment, waving goodbye to Morgana.

As soon as the door shuts, Morgana unzips her suitcase and takes out her clothes.

"So, you and Max, huh?" she asks.

"What do you mean?" I ask.

She meets my gaze with a grin. "You having him as a mentor? Meeting what sounds like more than once a week?"

"I can assure you it's just that. A communal mentorship."

"Mmhmm," she says with a smile while unpacking her suitcase.

"I'm serious, girl. There's nothing going on."

"I don't know how you do it though. With a body like that and those gray eyes? I'd be distracted all the time."

"Morgana!" I exclaim.

"It's true though!" she laughs while opening her dresser. "I'd love for him to be my mentor."

"Oh, my God, no. Just no," I say while placing her stationary on her desk.

In the back of my mind, I remember the feeling I had during our first meeting; me being nervous, feeling my cheeks redden as I tried my best to pretend that I read the self-defense chapter, forcing my mind to focus on the different spells.

Well, she does have a point.

"So, what's this B-floor Max mentioned?"

OCTOBER 31ST, 2018
"Dude, Religion is such a drag now!" I tell Morgana as we walk out of the largest lecture hall on campus. Everyone was eager to get out of there since we've pretty much been reviewing for the midterm next week. I can tell that midterm season

is in full swing as I can sense the stress and tension among everyone. Even though that religion class is so easy, all the other students in there are mostly south campus majors—known as STEM majors, like engineers and pre-med students.

I used to be a part of that community, but I learned that I hated biology and chemistry with a passion. I'd rather not waste my precious time doing things I hate, so I might as well stay a psychology major to keep things interesting. Just being in that lecture hall made me feel so stressed even though I only have a paper to write and the midterm for my psych research class. That's the one I am scared for. But I do hope I can do well.

"Just wish reviewing would be more interesting. I am so mad we don't have to know Wicca or the other earth-based religions for the midterm!" I feel a little frustrated that I have to memorize sacraments, historical facts, and God knows what else about the main religions.

"You know, I am gonna struggle the most, right?" Morgana exclaims as we head to the student union for lunch.

"Why? You seem to be… wait." I just realized she's a witch. Duh…

She gives me a smug grin. *Yeah, I totally forgot. Oops.*

"Look, I'll help you with Christianity and Catholicism and you can teach me more about Wicca for the final. It works out!"

"Yeah, that can work," Morgana replies.

We walk for a few moments in silence as we both clearly are stressing for midterms, plus we just want food so bad. I know I haven't eaten anything all morning and I am pretty sure Morgana hasn't either. We've been surviving on Veggie Grill for the past week and I am so sick of vegan "Chick'n Tenders." It's the most affordable option but I can tell that it's taking a toll on my body by making me feel bloated. I am definitely gonna tell Max that the other folks need to let us cook our vegan stuff.

After we get our lunches to go, we head off to our usual spot to chill. It's right in the center of campus on the hill by the notorious Janss Steps. It's pretty much a tourist spot that everyone loves to see since the tour guides take you all the way up an enormous number of stairs so that you can get to the top and yeah, take pictures. But you also get to scream. Your voice ends up echoing if you scream loud enough. Needless to say, elementary school kids get a huge kick out of it since they get to scream the loudest ever. That's why that spot may not be the best study spot. Morgana and I try to stay as far away from the main stairs as possible.

After we find a comfy spot, Morgana pulls out her tapestry for us to lie on. And yes, it has a neon purple pentagram on a black background. Usually, this tapestry alone is able to keep the "fanatical Christians" from talking to us for hours. I understand their intention of spreading the word of God by mouth, but when I just want to relax, I really don't want anyone bugging me.

Or us.

We love to have conversations about all kinds of things, and I'd rather not have some random person just cut us off. It happened once when Morgana was teaching me a spell on how to manifest my hopes and dreams. They are usually quiet and just leave, but I have a feeling this time was not going to be as quiet.

"So," Morgana ventures, "how's your meetings with Max? It's now what, three times a week?" She glances at me and lifts her brows with a grin

Oh, no, please, no.

"They're going really well. Been learning how to properly manage the self-defense spells," I say with a nervous laugh.

"Yeah, I heard you kicked his ass a little too hard with those spells."

"Oh, my God. It was an accident!" I exclaim. "It's my fault for not going over the spells."

"'Cause you were distracted, right?" Morgana says sarcastically.

"Really?" I exclaim while shaking my head.

"I told you. It was inevitable you would."

"No. It's my psych class that—"

"Mhmm." She glances back at me. "Poor Max got his ass kicked by his future girlfriend."

"You suck." I playfully smack her with my folder.

"Hey, don't get mad at me. I can tell there's something going on."

"Again. There's nothing going on."

"You guys are together, right? Because I can see the chemistry between—"

"Hi, you guys!" A random guy walks toward us, adjusting his red hat as he decides to sit near us. We both take one look at his hat, which is that one that is tied to racism and injustice that virtually everyone hates, and move back with our lunches in hand.

"You've gotta be kidding me," whispers Morgana under her breath.

This is not gonna end well. Typically, people wearing this hat support a political party that is very Christian-oriented.

"How are you?" he asks.

"Fine before you got here," says Morgana, clearly mad this random guy decided to cut in.

"Look, we're really busy and can't talk about religion right now. We're actually tired of it since we've been reviewing Christianity all morning," I say politely, hoping the guy would leave.

"That's a damn shame. I'm the one of the main coordinators of *a Christian org known as Alpha Tau Chi, or ATX for short,* and am hoping we can talk about the miracles God gives us like the trees and food like cows that give us really good burgers," he replies.

"Well, we're actually vegan," I say gesturing to the two of us. Meanwhile, Morgana keeps trying to find the larger pentagram to scare him away.

"Dammit," Morgana says as she rummages in her bag.

"You vegans really love to save the planet, right? Did you know that God put those cows on this planet to be eaten? That's why we have these canines here," he says, pointing to his teeth. *Damn. He really wants to start an argument.*

"Look, I'd rather not argue over veganism in general. Can you please leave?" I ask even though I am attempting to stifle any sign of anger in my voice.

"This world is gonna fall apart because of you libtards, ya know that?" he says while adjusting his hat, clearly trying to convey a political statement. *Oh, no.*

Finally, Morgana saves me by pulling out her athame, an iridescent curved knife, with a big pentagram on it, usually used to remove negative energy ties people can place on others. She also removes her black shawl, revealing the large pentagram tattoo on her chest.

"Leave us alone and take your political shit for brains out of here," she says while holding the athame in her lap.

"You satanic bitch," he yells at us and I feel so uncomfortable. "What? Are you gonna stab me with that demonic blade?"

She attempts to remain calm. I am scared shitless, yet she seems collected. How?

"Like I said before," she says while staring down at her athame, turning it over to admire its beauty. "You can just leave us alone and nothing bad will happen, okay?"

"Is that a threat?" he asks.

Morgana shakes her head. "Don't you know what witches are?"

"Demonic bitches trying to achieve dominance since they'll never be as superior as us men?" he asks.

Morgana laughs while admiring the shiny look given to her athame by the sunlight. "We are capable of so much." She looks up at Red Hat. "We can do spells, magic." Suddenly, I hear rustling behind me. Red Hat looks behind us, fear in his eyes. The rustling continues.

"The one piece of advice I can give you," she says while leaning forward, athame in her hand. She's about a mere centimeters away from his face. "Never fuck with a witch," she whispers to him.

All of a sudden, I feel a strong gust of wind blow my hair forward followed by the numerous popping sounds. I brush my hair away and see the guy being pelted by pinecones. He tries to stand and shield himself with his arm but falls back down.

Morgana moves back, laughing as the tall guy is left struggling with a bunch of pinecones coming at him from out of nowhere. He's defenseless and it's so funny to see him being pelted. I know it's bad, but this is too funny.

"I hope you rot in hell, you freak!" he yells while running away.

"Well, I don't believe in hell nor Satan so screw off," Morgana says as she laughs, seeing him scared out of his mind.

I am still in shock even though I laughed at that asshole getting beat up by pinecones.

"Wait." I realize in shock. I look around, hoping no one else saw what we just did. "Did anyone see?" I ask, on the verge of having an anxiety attack. The one rule we can't break is revealing our true powers. If anyone sees it, captures it on video, and posts it somewhere, we're totally screwed.

Morgana shakes her head. "This is why I chose the area partly in the shade, high up the hill by the bushes here. Nobody is willing to walk all the way up here unless they wanna start something." She puts her athame away and resumes eating her burrito.

Wow. "I have so much to learn from you." I grin.

"You know," she says. "It takes like major strength to pelt an asshole with pinecones."

I laugh so hard. Lunch on this hill is always interesting.

"But I do have to ask. Why is your athame in your backpack?" I grab a few fries.

She shrugs. "Never know when you gotta cut that negativity outta your life."

"Just for the record," I say while taking my last bite of lunch. "You make me wanna become a witch 'cause you empower me to embrace that freak side of us."

Morgana smiles.

"And that's why you make an awesome roommate." I smile, loving the positive vibes we have right now.

After a few moments of silence, Morgana again asks the dreaded question I've been avoiding. "So you and Max are together, right?"

NOVEMBER 15TH, 2018

I knock twice on Max's door, letting him know of my arrival for the weekly meetings. I am so nervous since the incident over the weekend. I didn't think the throwing back spell would throw him that far. He ended up getting thrown across the room, luckily with no injuries. But of course, Avi happened to just walk in at the right moment, seeing Max flying.

I really didn't think word would spread this fast though. It's barely Monday, and the group chat is highly active because of it. Normally, Max and I don't meet on Mondays, but I needed to apologize in person. I really should've paid more attention to both the spells and the spell casting itself.

Suddenly, the door opens and I step back as the Lunar Twins walking out. Max calls after them to be careful again. Morgana has been trying to help them, given that they both are trained by the head witch, but they're still struggling. So there will always be meetings with them and Max. I take a deep breath to calm my nerves that are way too active out of embarrassment.

"Hey, come on in." Max stands in the doorway, gesturing for me to come in.

"Hey," I say as I walk in, feeling my cheeks warm as I take a seat on the couch, briefly taking out my phone to pretend to answer text messages in order to temporarily distract myself.

He sits down on the couch and puts his phone away.

"I'm so sorry about this weekend. I didn't think it'd turn out that way," I say at last, meeting his gaze.

"It's fine. Accidents happen all the time. I'm actually impressed how you used the *rediro* spell though."

Oh, thank God. "Really?"

He nods. "Most beginners struggle with that one and have trouble making the spell work. In your case, you've pretty much mastered it."

"At the time, I thought I was doing it right. I've struggled keeping up with the readings so I thought the spell wouldn't work at all."

He shakes his head. "The book gives you an overall guide on how to use it but the main part, which is casting the spell itself, involves practice with a mentor and your own intuition. Those are more important than just the book alone."

"Okay, cool." I sigh and briefly glance at the floor. "I just wanted to say that to you in person rather than over text."

"Yeah, that's understandable. We can go over it more tomorrow along with the attack spells so you'll be fine."

"Sounds good." I briefly check my phone, Morgana sent me a text reminding me of our study session we planned for our midterm. "I totally forgot I have a study session with Morgana for our midterm, so I have to head out. But I'll see you tomorrow." I get up from the couch, heading for the door.

"Oh, Cur, before you leave," Max says right before I open the door. "Do you have plans for Friday night?"

I shake my head. "No, I don't think so." *What is he gonna ask?*

"Do you wanna have dinner with me in Westwood? We can go wherever is cool with you."

Wait. Is this a date?

"Yeah," I say with a smile, feeling my cheeks warm.

"Perfect. I'll text you the time and everything else later on this week."

"That sounds good."

"Alrighty. I'll see you Friday night."

Did Max Gray just ask me out?

CHAPTER 6

DECEMBER 2ND, 2018
3 p.m.

It's been a couple weeks but so much has happened. I've managed to get The Community's garden back to life and have made a few more friends so Morgana and I have our own circle of friends now. Turns out the Lunar Twins are pretty cool witches to have as friends. Finals are already approaching fast, and I've been up to my neck in studying, reading more about Witchcraft and Curanderismo while also managing to care of the apartment itself.

But here's the best thing that's happened all quarter: Max and I started dating. This is something I never thought I'd end up doing. We've still been having meetings about learning different spells while also trying to figure out what my main power is, which is still an ongoing mission. However, I may be able to find some more support for this.

I decided to do more research in the Latin American studies library and found a book similar to the one in The Community except it describes historical findings of *Curanderos* that were mostly deemed as folk tales that originated in Mexico, but nothing more. I spoke with the librarian for about two hours on how to find one, but they said it's almost impossible since there's little to no evidence of them recorded in Mexico. Through oral tradition, it's said that they only reveal their powers to whom they deem are worthy. I'm guessing this means being gifted like me, though I am not exactly sure.

It just so happens we have about three weeks of winter break but if I need more time, I will take time off from school. It's just something I need to do. I need to go on this journey to discover more about my powers and honestly more about myself.

I plan on telling both Max and Morgana tonight and start planning for the trip. It's scary having to venture off on this journey but I know I have to.

9 p.m.

"So Catholicism has angels and saints but other forms of Christianity don't?" Morgana asks while reviewing our notes for the final.

"Yes. Those angels and saints usually have specific purposes that people can call upon to assist them with whatever area of their life they need it in."

"So, it's kind of like confiding in archetypes of the God and Goddess, like The Green Man or Aphrodite for specific purposes, but they are all still apart of the God and Goddess?"

"Yeah," I reply as Morgana flips through her notes.

"Can we take a break?" Morgana asks while closing her notebook. "This section is really gonna be tough to manage on the final."

"You'll be fine. I'll help you as much as I can and at the end of the day, this is still a GE so it shouldn't be difficult. The midterm was a breeze and I'm sure this will be."

"I just wish winter break was here already," she says while glancing at her succulent terrarium. "What are your plans for break?"

"Well, I'm actually going to Mexico."

"Mexico?" she asks.

I nod. "I need to go to help get guidance on what my powers are. They're tied to a form of Mexican magic that I need a better understanding of to discover that part of me. I also just need to go out and find myself out there, you know?"

She nods. "That makes total sense. You'll come back after break though, right?"

I pause for a moment and stare at my Curanderismo book. "If it needs more than three weeks, I might take time off winter quarter."

"What?!" she exclaims. "You're really willing to miss a quarter?"

I nod. "Whatever it takes. I need to do this. It's something I can't keep holding back from. Even though my Spanish might not be the best, I'll adapt to it."

"Wow. That's amazing though."

I nod while meeting her gaze. "I'm pretty excited about all of this."

"Wait. Is there anything else you've been doing behind the scenes lately that I don't know about? I didn't know anything about this trip in the making."

I smile. "You already know."

"Oh, my God!" she exclaims. "It makes total sense. I've seen the way you look at each other during The Community Meetings. You're pretty much gone all the time from the apartment and you've been a lot happier recently."

"Wow. You sure notice a lot," I reply. "We should get back to—"

"Screw studying. I wanna hear more," she says.

"Well, we'd both rather not tell anyone because we felt that, you know—"

"That it might seem so soon since you've only known him for like six weeks," she says.

"Exactly. Plus I didn't want it to seem like I'm messing with the head of the apartment to get excused from a lot of things," I say with a grin.

"That's so damn true," Morgana replies with sudden realization. "You lucky ass!" she says while playfully pushing me. "You probably don't have to do any chores because you can just give him something, ya know what I'm saying," she says in a pseudo-seductive voice.

"Stop," I tell her.

"My girl is with the head of The Community. My Goddess, woman, you scored. Also, I am low-key happy I have you as a roommate because of this."

"Why?" I ask.

"I know you're gonna spend a lot more time on the first floor," she replies, arching her eyebrow.

"My God, Morgana, I am so not!"

"Honestly, girl, embrace that slutty side of you. There's nothing wrong with getting some. You should know being a part of that sex club."

"Hey! It's a sexual health education club. Not just one big orgy."

"Mmhmm sure."

I roll my eyes.

DECEMBER 27TH, 2018

AEROPUERTO INTERNACIONAL DE LA CIUDAD DE MÉXICO

I clutch my backpack as close as possible. I love Mexico so much, yet my anxiety tells me to constantly watch my stuff and my back. It's probably just traveling anxiety. It's so unfortunate my Spanish is not the greatest. If only I knew how to ask for a taxi or bus or some type of transportation.

I try asking someone where the bus is, but of course, I butcher it way too much, and the man walks away, confused. I ask another woman where the taxi is and again, another confused look. I ask yet another person with the same thing happening. I finally just give up.

I find a seat on a nearby bench and place my head in my hands, admitting defeat. I knew this was so not a good plan. Traveling to Mexico all on my own, hoping to gain some clarity. Those people in movies make it look so damn easy; that they can find themselves just by taking a risk and doing something so drastic like this. I figured returning to my homeland may give me some insight not only about powers but also about what my true life purpose is.

Now it seems as if I just got myself into some big mess. Although I can just try to get a plane ticket back and leave this place, something is itching for me to stay. I don't know why, considering I just spontaneously decided to do this. This may have been an extremely bad idea. Tears start to flow. I feel so damn lost right now. Not just in Mexico, but my *life*.

As I let the tears flow, I feel someone near me. My instincts kick in. I wipe my eyes clean and grab my backpack close to me. I don't trust anyone—not even the old man who I noticed took a seat near me. I shake my head, contemplating getting a return ticket home. This may have been the worst idea in my life.

The old man near me asks, *"Mija, estas bien?"* Am I okay? *Definitely not.* But I nod. I turn to the man and tell him I am fine and that my Spanish isn't perfect, that I wasn't fluent at all.

I notice the man wears glasses, a tropical pattern shirt, and the most comfortable shoes on the planet known in Mexican culture: *Huaraches,* or Mexican sandals—the English translations does not do it justice at all. He looks like he could be someone's grandpa. He gives off such a welcoming vibe though, unlike any that I have felt ever since I got off the plane.

"That's okay, *Mija*. I know some English. It may not be perfect though," he replies in a thick Spanish accent.

I could not be happier. "Thank goodness! I've been so lost. I thought my minimal Spanish would just magically improve being here. I've been trying to ask someone for a bus or taxi."

He nods. "That can be a hard thing to do with a new language. Do you know where you need to take the bus to?"

I shake my head. "Uhh. I don't know why I came here. I thought that coming here… I'd be able to find myself."

"Ah," he replies. "I know a lot of people who try to find out who they are." He looks off in the distance, silent for a few moments, as if he's contemplating something. "If you need help, I can help with that."

"Yeah, I can definitely use a translator. Hopefully, I can find a hotel—"

"Oh, no, *Mija,* I can help with more than just translating. I can help you find yourself." He gets up from his seat, picking up a messenger bag from his side. He looks down at me. "*Mija,* you have so much power within you but you can't see it. I can help you see that power."

Although I feel like I should trust this man, the horror stories of kidnapping and ransom come to mind. I am extremely hesitant.

"I am sorry, but I don't know if I can trust you. Not in a mean way, of course, but I don't know if that's a good idea."

He sits down, then looks side to side as if making sure no one is looking. He closes his eyes for a brief moment, cupping his hands and saying something incoherent under his breath. He opens his eyes and stares down at his hands. He gently opens them, revealing a soft yellow glow. It appears to be a ball of light, with white clouds swirling around it like a water globe.

Suddenly, the ball changes colors from bright yellow to a dark green. It begins to morph, the light particles shifting into a small oval shape. Then there's red light, then white and blue. Within seconds, the particles came together, revealing a bird. It's beautiful. With green plumage, a red chest, and white feathers. But what makes it unique is the long green tail feather.

Wait. That bird looks *so* familiar. But I just can't seem to remember what it's called. I am in awe, shocked and frozen to my chair as I witness the beauty of this mystery man's magic.

"This is a quetzal, one of the creators of this land," he says while holding the mini-quetzal in his palm. He stokes the bird softly, as if it's his pet. "And you, *mija*…" He looks up at me. "You can call to him and all the deities above. I can show you how."

He closes his hands, and the bird disappears out of thin air. That bird was solid but now it's just gone like dust. He has magical powers just like The Community back home. I need to go with him. There's just something there.

"I wanna know how," I reply.

He nods. "Very well. I can provide you a place to stay, food, everything. And I will teach you how to harvest your true powers. Follow me." He rises from the bench and picks up his messenger bag.

"Thank you so much, *Señor.*"

"You're welcome, *mija*. And you can call me Quetzal. *Señor* makes me feel so old," he says with a chuckle.

I place my backpack on my shoulders and follow him through the airport. He manages to find a taxi just as it arrives at the pickup zone right outside. The taxi ride is pretty calm. Quiet at least on my side given the fact that I can only understand parts of the conversation Quetzal is having with the driver. I decide to look out the window as Mexico City flashes by. So many unrecognizable buildings and names that I will definitely not be able to remember.

JANUARY 28ᵀᴴ, 2019

CHIHUAHUA DESERT COMMUNITY, MEXICO

It's been about a month since I arrived in Quetzal's hometown. He's actually part of an indigenous community that lives a few hours out from Mexico City in the Chihuahua Desert. The community has been so welcoming of me despite being an outsider. Quetzal said that they know the hidden power I have and that I am capable of helping in so many ways while also having the calling to share their wisdom with me.

Tonight, there's a tradition tribal event aimed at asking Pachamama to bring back the seasonal rain that is needed to keep the crops growing in order to sustain life—not only for the villagers but also to bring Mother Earth back to its healthy state. It's unfortunate Quetzal can only travel to the city to obtain as much supplies as necessary for the village but can only go on certain times of the year. This time, he went into Mexico City, which is about a two-hour drive in search of these supplies. However, he had a calling to come to the airport where I would be. He knew that he had to go to that airport to eventually meet me as he said that I have immense power that can potentially help the village and much more.

Once we arrived, he told me the creation story that was mentioned in the books that I've read before and that I myself may be that special *Curandera* given my abilities to resurrect the plants, but we've been having some difficulty in trying to help me to resurrect the crops. Every time I try to bring back a sprout from the ground back to life, it ends up growing a little bit then withering back, something that didn't happen before. I'm guessing my powers only last so long.

I feel the heat of the fire against my skin as I sit by the campfire waiting for the ceremony to start.

Suddenly, the children of the village begin dancing around the fire as the elders engage in a music ensemble of flutes and drums. I gently sway side to side, trying to engage in the ceremony, but the thoughts of my failed attempts with my power fill my mind, bringing me to the verge of tears of frustration and anger. I get up and walk away back toward

Quetzal's home and arrive at my bedroom near the back of the house.

I sit down on the bed and glance at the texts, wondering how weeks of reading that gave me exercises to help my powers didn't help at all. Quetzal's wisdom passed down from generations of Curanderos didn't help either. I wipe the tears from my face as I place the texts on the table next to my notebook. I wish my phone got reception out here so I could call up Morgana and vent to her. It's moments like these when I feel like just giving up. This trip had to have been a big mistake. I walk back to my bed and shake my head, wiping more tears and sniffling. I glance from the window, the vast darkness contrasting with the orange light of the lanterns near the windowsill, then to my agave succulent.

Quetzal found this one bright green succulent right outside the village, the only plant that is bright green out of all the plants in this desert that stretches for miles. He gave this plant to me as a reminder of what I am capable of and my love for nature. I pick up the pot with the succulent and feel the smoothness of the leaves, admiring how it somehow survived out in this heat that even succulents may not survive in. I think that it may use some water since it's been maybe about a week since I've watered it. I reach for a water bottle nearby to give it some water and I feel my hands are really sweaty. Although the heat is not as bad at night, I'm not drenched anywhere else on my body.

Maybe I spilled some water beforehand. I put the water bottle down and reach for the nearby towel at the end of the bed and rub my hands on it, making sure that my hands are dry and reach for the water bottle again. The same thing happens with my hands still wet even though I made sure they were dry.

This is weird.

I dry them once more, giving up on trying to water my succulent and walk over to the desk, hoping to get my mind off it by reading the text. I open it to the page I bookmarked.

> *...Ometeotl, the divine energy all things contain, a truth to their being that unites them in Their divine essence. This story does not tell us of the birth of the "god" of the sun, but rather of the birth of the Sun Himself...*

Suddenly, I notice the pages begin to darken as the water on my hands damage the book. I immediately close it and dry my hands on my pants and open my hand.

This can't be real.

Water starts dripping down from my fingertips, three small streams of water flowing from my fingertips down my palm and my arm, the water dripping down onto the floor. I feel the same stream of water on my right arm and I lift up palms facing me, streams of water flowing through both. I am too frozen in shock to react fast enough to reach for the towel until I see the water forming a small pool on the floor.

I run toward the bathroom and flick the water into the sink. Wait. Water streams down my fingertips into the sink almost like a faucet but not as powerful. I hear Quetzal call from the front door.

"*Mija. Donde estas?*" he asks where I am since I am usually at the ceremonies.

I meet his gaze as he approaches the doorway, lifting my hands up over the sink, letting him see the water flowing through my fingertips.

"You have a lot more power than I thought," he replies.

FEBRUARY 10TH, 2019
I'm out in the garden preparing for another exercise on channeling my energy in hopes of recreating the water scene from a few days ago. We're hoping that the grounding exercise today will help me control the water power I have so that it doesn't surprise me unexpectedly anymore. I've tried on my own to recreate it but I can't seem to get the water to flow. It's like I always encounter some block whenever I try channeling it. Luckily, my power to bring back the plants is a lot better with more grounding exercises that allow me to no longer doubt my abilities. I can now bring the plants back to life from a distance instead of having to physically touch them.

I put my palms out in front of me and begin channeling the energy, feeling the heat rise from my arms all the way to the top of my head and down through my body. I notice the stalks of corn begin to turn green, leaves slowly begin to rise. The corn itself begins turning back to its yellow color. I manage to bring these back and I hope they stay this way. I walk toward the corn and gently squeeze it, making sure that it's stable. Suddenly, I feel a cold sensation in my hands, as if I placed my hand in a refrigerator. I pull my hand away and feel the water streaming down my hands down the stock into the soil below.

I bend down toward the bottom of the stalks and place my hands out front. The stream of water soaks the soil, the smell of wet dirt filling my nostrils. In the back of my mind, I hear a voice saying *water* repeatedly, almost like a mantra. I do want to water all the corn stalks, so I repeat that mantra over and over with the intention of helping these plants grow. As I recite the mantra in my mind, the water continues to stream out of my hand as I walk around all the corn stalks, making sure the soil is watered enough to keep these guys alive. Okay. I'm done watering and I want the water to stop now. I say stop a few times. Immediately, the water stops and I dry my hands on my pants.

Quetzal walks out of the back door, clanking metal. He is carrying the watering can and I meet his gaze.

"We don't need it anymore," I say as I rise up from the ground.

"The water thing happened again, huh?"

I nod. "This time, I used your grounding and intention practice and a voice came up in the back of my mind, repeating the word *water* a few times and I started repeating it like a mantra."

"And what did you do to stop it?"

"I made sure to say *stop* out loud and in my head to make sure I'm able to keep it under control."

He nods. "I'm guessing the distant channeling with the plants worked too, right?" He glances at the corn stalks then back to me.

"Yeah. That's improving too. I'm really hoping my powers will get better from here on out."

"They definitely will." Quetzal looks off into the distance.

FEBRUARY 27TH, 2019

We walk over a few yards away from Quetzal's house to a dry, rocky basin with cracks in the dirt due to severe dehydration.

Suddenly, Quetzal stops near a small rocky hill. I look over and see a dry crack that's about three feet long and about a foot wide that's on a slight incline down and then flattens out at the bottom.

"What's the exercise today?" I ask.

"We'll be practicing your water abilities further. Here's what I want you to do." He crouches toward the top of the hill and places his hand on the dirt. "I want you to place your hands at the top here and do exactly what you did before when you watered my crops. I want you to channel that energy using that intention of saying *water* in the back of your mind. I'll tell you when to stop channeling so that you can gain better control of it."

"Okay." I walk over to the spot Quetzal begins to walk away from.

I close my eyes, take a deep breath, and place my hands on the ground. In my mind, I tell myself the phrase *water this earth* and repeat the water mantra while focusing on my hands and channeling all my energy into it. Suddenly, I feel the cold sensation in my hands like before and I continue repeating *water* over and over again. I begin to feel the ground moisten, the smell of wet dirt filling my nostrils. I open my eyes and gently lift my hands, streams of water flowing from my fingertips down the crack toward the bottom.

I've created a river with my own hands.

MARCH 15TH, 2019

I watch the sunset over the distant hills as the pink and orange hues of the clouds begin to darken; bright blue and white stars begin to shine. I smile, admiring the beauty of the desert, how Mother Nature is capable of creating the vibrant colors that kiss the horizon, followed by the stars at night. I'm usually buried in the texts Quetzal has given me, learning the infinite knowledge and history of the Aztecs, from their healing modalities to the creation of the Warriors and Earth Saviors.

I still can't believe I possess the power of multiple elements. Quetzal has said that most Curanderos can only have power over one of them that takes years to learn. Yet, I have the power of two of them at twenty years old. That's impressive power right there.

I glance at my watch, noticing it's 7:30 p.m. Quetzal and I have a practice exercise with candles tonight. He usually engages in candle magic to help the villagers with healing, preparing the candles similar to how The Community does back home. He even has his own version of the Apothecary near the front of the house where the villagers come to him for healing of their ailments.

I head over to the candle room, noticing the darkness inside with faint orange light. I walk in and see Quetzal grabbing an unlit white glass candle from a cabinet, placing it near the green one with a large flame flickering.

"Am I doing a candle spell?" I ask.

He shakes his head. "We're going to test to see if you have any other abilities with the other elements. Today we'll be testing fire."

He grabs a dish and puts in underneath the unlit candle and walks away from the table, gesturing for me to stand in front of the candles.

"I want you to light the candle."

How in the world am I supposed to do this? I only control plants and water, which are the complete opposite of fire.

"I don't know if I can do this but I'll try." I look at the candle, the unlit wick protruding from the white wax.

"I'll guide you along the way. First, I want you to close your eyes and hold your palms in front of you as if you were bringing the plants back."

I do as he says while taking a few deep breaths to relax me.

"I want you to envision the colors red and orange, the colors of fire, in the back of your mind, imagining large flames that rise up to the sky."

I imagine the fire from the ceremony in the middle of the village, seeing the flames rising high above, the embers falling down near the rocks at the bottom controlling the fire.

"Now, I want to you to envision the candle in front of you. Imagine the wick slowly glowing as the flame rises."

I visualize the rising of the flame just like the candles I used to light.

"Now channel your energy into the candle in front of you, envision the candle lighting, feeling the heat of the fire against your skin, how the color of the flame lights up the room."

I begin channeling my energy, feeling the flame slowly growing, flickering and reaching higher until it comes back down to its original small flame. Suddenly, I feel the heat I get while channeling, except this time, the heat is a lot warmer. It feels as if I'm putting my hand near the heat of a stove. I open my eyes as I feel this heat go from my hand, down my arms, toward the candle. The wick slowly starts to glow with a small flame rising until it dips back down to a small, steady flame flickering in the darkness.

"Amazing." Quetzal approaches the white candle I just lit. "Even though it's a small flame you've created, this is immense power."

I feel the heat sensation cool as I step backward, admiring the flickering of the flame. "I still can't believe I did this." I glance up to Quetzal. "I never imagined I'd be capable of this, the water, and the plants." I smile while meeting Quetzal's gaze.

"I knew you had immense power when I met you. You're capable of managing three out of the four elements at such a young age; earth when you bring the crops back, water with the small stream you created and now this." He gestures toward the candle. "And fire. You have a power that transcends all types of Curanderos."

"I thought there were three main lineages with different types of Curanderos from the healers to the Earth Saviors?" I ask.

"There are, but you can master three of the five total elements."

"Wait. I though there were four elements?"

"There are four of the earth, three of which you can master, and there's one more that no human has ever been able to master—and that's spirit."

"Spirit? Oh, so it's like the pentagram with the five elements, right?"

He nods. "Every culture has their variation so that would be the Celtic take on it, while we have the ancestral lineages and Aztec deities."

"That makes sense."

"And so mastering the spirit element, which so far has seemed impossible for centuries, would allow humans to travel into the spirit realm directly and be able to bring the spirits into the physical world. You'd also be able to communicate directly with the Gods and be able to enter their sacred realm. No one has ever done this. But whoever does encompass the power of all the existing elements, will be known as *Pentalpha,* the one above all."

He looks away for a moment then back to me. "Given that you've mastered three of the total elements at such a young age, there's a chance that you may be able to master spirit too."

"And become *Pentalpha*?"

He nods

I am silent for a moment and look off into the distance.

Me. The one above all even the elements of nature and spirit? There's no way that's me. *Or is it?*

"I want to see if I can master all of the elements." I meet Quetzal's gaze. "How would I do that?"

He sighs. "That's unfortunately out of my area of teaching, *Mija*. Even the air element is something that the Curanderos I know who have taught me weren't capable of."

I look back to the candle, taking all the information in. "I guess I'd have to figure that out myself, right?"

He nods. "You'll have to take the knowledge that I have given you to delve deeper into your powers by practicing through grounding and intentions. You can take all the texts I have to help you, even those written in Nauhatl, which, as you know, is the language of the ancient Aztec tribes. I know you'll be able to learn how to understand it all."

I'm quiet for a few moments, grateful to have made it this far with my powers. I meet Quetzal's gaze. "Thank you for being my mentor and for helping me through this. I don't know how to repay you."

"No need, *Mija*. You've brought the greatest gift of all by allowing me to mentor you and allow you to see the power you have. You're going to do great things back home."

MARCH 26TH, 2019

It's my last day before I head back to the airport and back to The Community in Westwood. I've learned a lot out here with Quetzal and his community of tribal leaders who have welcomed me and taught me about so many things: about myself, my powers, and my life journey. I will miss this place so much.

I pack my backpack with all the books and folders containing Quetzal's texts, my clothes, and the gift the villagers gave me that will always be near and dear to my heart: a flute carved out of clay with the air piece shaped like a serpent and a round top etched with lines to resemble the plumage that's painted green. The color contrasts against the clay, the mouth carved in and painted white, and blue flames on both eyes upward.

They call it *Tlapitzalli Mexica Coatl*. The flute of the serpent. This symbolizes the knowledge the elders gave to me while learning how to play music, something I've always dreamed of doing. And now, with this knowledge, I can take it with me along my journey. I place the flute back in its wooden box and back in my backpack.

"You ready?" Quetzal asks from the doorway.

"Yeah." I place the bag on my shoulders and walk out of the room toward the front door. The entire tribe waves goodbye to me as I walk toward his truck located near the edge of the village at the very spot where I stepped off, nervous and scared out of my mind having traveled out here into the desert not knowing what would happen, scared of taking this risk.

Now, looking back, I'm glad I took that risk.

I place my backpack in the backseat then jump in the front seat as Quetzal turns the ignition. I take a quick glance in the rear view mirror, seeing all the green grass, succulents, and crops I helped bring back for the village that I called home these past few months.

"You've brought life back to my village," Quetzal says while looking back in the rear view mirror. We glance at each other. "That is the best gift you could've ever given us."

5 p.m. Aeropuerto Internacional de la Ciudad de México

Quetzal rolls to a stop outside of the airport behind the line of cars dropping off people heading into terminal three. As I get out of the truck, taking my backpack from the backseat, Quetzal walks around to my side and hugs me.

"*Gracias, para todo, Mija. Cuídate.*" He thanks me for everything and wishes me a safe journey.

"Thank you for everything, Quetzal. I'll miss you so much." I walk toward the terminal waving goodbye, my eyes watering as I stand in line waiting to pass the security screening.

8 p.m.

As I wait for the time to board, I turn on my phone, seeing a slew of messages everyone sent while I was gone. Even though there's so many, I respond to Max first. He asks to call and I check the time, making sure that I have a half hour until boarding and let him call.

"Hey," I say with a smile.

"Hey, babe. It's been so long since I've heard your voice."

"Same. I miss you so much. I wish I was home already but I have another three hours to get through," I reply.

"Okay, you'll be coming in around midnight then, right?"

"Yeah. It'll be the same terminal you dropped me off at."

"Perfect. I'll be there waiting. Just let me know when you land."

"Will do."

"I can't wait to see you. I have a surprise for you when you get back."

"Now I really wish I was there already," I say with a laugh. Suddenly, I hear the announcement for boarding. "Hey, I gotta go. I'm boarding now. I'll see you in a few hours."

We both say goodbye and I put my phone in my pocket.

Let's head home.

CHAPTER 7

Meanwhile, back in Westwood, Los Angeles

MARCH 24TH, 2019, 11 P.M.
"You, guys! It's midnight. SCREAM!" Everyone erupts in screaming, whooping, and yelling. It's the traditional finals week yell.

Everyone at UCLA does it, although it's a lot cooler in the dorms rather than the apartments. You have to be mindful of the neighbors who aren't all students. So, yeah, that's a drag. What isn't much of a drag is the fact that Chad Westin decided that studying at Powell had finally drained him, so he decided to take a walk back to his apartment, which of course, was in a frat known as Phi Delta Rho.

Studying there was so useless because he knew full well that all of the frat boys were just going to be smoking weed, playing drinking games like rage cage, beer pong, and pretty much everything else aside from actually studying. It sucked that he couldn't live on the hill 'cause now his walk was more like twenty minutes, or like a five-minute bird ride, but where in the hell were all the birds at this hour? At the frats, where they were victim to deranged drunk guys trying to "relax" right before finals. Well, it's hell week already and biochemistry wasn't going to learn itself.

It's too bad that his apartment is in pretty much darkness but that wasn't going to make finals feel better. In fact, it made things worse. If only there was something that could cheer good ole Chad up.

As he crosses the street, waiting at the crosswalk, he notices someone sitting at the bus stop. It's a woman wearing a fur coat and in red heels that hint at some promiscuity. She has this presence of power, making his attraction to her undeniable, although it's hard to see her face given the dark fedora covering her head. He wishes he could see her rather than just look at her red high heels. He needs to figure out who or what this woman is doing at this hour.

"Excuse me, uh, are you lost or something? I'm sure there aren't any buses coming anytime soon."

She turns around, taking off her fedora, revealing beauty that is unfathomable. With ruby red lips, wavy scarlet hair and bright blue eyes, she is… beautiful.

He can't take his eyes off her.

"I am waiting." She stares across the street at a neighboring frat. She reaches into her coat and pulls out a cigarette, followed by a lighter.

"Are you waiting for someone?"

She looks at him, quickly looking him over head to toe. Then looks straight at the frat across the street. "There's a guy in that frat. Owes me some money." She takes a drag from her cigarette. "He needs to come out. Otherwise…"

"Otherwise what?

"You're a funny one." She moves in her seat, revealing bright red lingerie covering her body. She is pretty young too, probably no more than twenty-two. *But what is she doing here?*

"I'm just a little worried for you. The frats can get pretty rowdy. And you shouldn't be out at this hour. But—"

"I can take care of myself. But I must wait."

"I can't let you do that alone. If you need someone to walk with, I can—"

"Shut it." She gets up from the bench.

"But you shouldn't be out—"

"Shh." She approaches him and places a finger to his lips to silence him. Within an instant, his thoughts go from concern to… *lust*. He notices her lithe body. Curvaceous, thick in the areas he likes.

Wait.

He shouldn't be thinking about that. Despite his girlfriend, who has been giving him crap for *accidentally* staring at her hot friend for a good solid five seconds, he must remain loyal. But this mystery woman looks so *damn* enticing.

She looks him up and down once more, her face covered in full face makeup and those red lips. "You're missing something in your life. I sense you have someone in your life who doesn't fulfill…" She opens up her coat more, getting closer to him.

He can smell her perfume, sweet with a hint of cinnamon. She leans in close, Chad is too shocked, too wrapped up in lust to move.

She whispers in his ear, "…your needs."

Chad *never* does things like this. *Random sex with a stranger?* She places her finger on his throat and trails it down slowly. Down until… He can't take this anymore. He can't think right. He… must…

She drags him along, crossing the street. They find a dark alleyway. Everything unfolds relatively quickly. Chad experiences the best pleasure he has ever known. Has the time of his life. After a few seconds of undeniable pleasure, the woman grips his throat, grabbing it harder and harder. Until his eyes roll back, his lifeless body falling to the ground.

The woman grabs her fur coat from the ground and opens her mirror. Within seconds, her appearance changes. She is now in sweatpants, sweatshirt, and sneakers. Her fur coat transforms into a small fur shawl. Her hair is no longer scarlet but dark brown. She pulls out her phone from her sweatpants pocket and sees text messages from her boyfriend Harden.

She immediately runs off, back to the dorms. She turns around, making sure no one had seen her. She loves the thrill of seducing these men, who sometimes are just innocent little angels, or are complete assholes, who are good riddance to this planet.

Lucius will be so pleased. All these innocent souls for him to consume, to become more powerful so that she can become the most powerful witch on the planet. He can give her that if she submits to the Dark Shadow Lord.

Poor Chad Westin.

The Night Killer got him.

MARCH 25TH, 2019, 3 P.M.

"Everyone, meeting in the common room, ASAP," Max barks at The Community members who just arrived back from class. He turns to his phone and sends a mass message to the entire building via text. He really should've invested in that intercom. Everyone begins to flood in, taking seats on the floor, the couch. A look of concern is etched on everyone's faces. There's a tension in the air that's palpable. It's a Wednesday afternoon during finals week, a time in which no meetings were to take place. Yet it has to for the sake of all The Community members.

"Okay, not everyone is here but this will do," says Max as he takes his place in the front of the room behind the podium. "So you all have probably heard of news or potential rumors from the nearby frats. It turns out one of the members of PDR was killed. They found his body in an alleyway between some apartments not too far from here."

"I hear it was by the abandoned Lutheran church right behind frat row," says Avi who is known to DJ at all the frats.

"Well, that's probably where it happened," Max says. "Either way, the police are scrambling to find a motive because it clearly was someone who had strangled him to death."

"This ain't good," muttered someone in the crowd.

Max tries to keep his cool. "I am seriously hoping none of y'all decided to do some wicked magic like that, but I am guessing nobody was out around 1 a.m. yesterday aside from Avi. Now I am not even considering Avi as a suspect because the police noticed bruise marks that may have been done by a woman."

Everyone starts to whisper, looking around trying to find some answers.

Morgana leans in the doorway, looking at the chaos of conversations emerge all around. "Hasn't Leo been able to figure out who it is?"

Max shakes his head. "There's no way he can. He's been trying all afternoon as soon as the news emerged on the *Daily Bruin*. Some type of block is present and that can only have been done by a powerful figure or force."

Will looks down, thinking. "You don't think The Council would send someone to do it. We are expecting them really soon."

Max shakes his head. "They wouldn't set foot over here unless they had a reason to. And death is punishable by that same offense, so they wouldn't even attempt to kill a mortal. But this is concerning because The Council may be able to see it and decide to investigate. I do not want them setting foot here. That would cause some major ass drama that could potentially get this safe haven shut down."

"What about Curanda?" Sabrina has always hated Curanda and even more after she got with Max.

"Sabrina." Max eyes her with a looks like he's fed up with her drama. "She's in Mexico right now. You honestly think she'd come over here just to kill? No, just—" He shakes his head in disbelief. "The reason I called this meeting is for you all to be on the look out and make sure you don't tell *anyone* if they ask that it's supernatural or magical-related. Keep your protective amulets on you and try your best to avoid those hate groups. They are definitely gonna be on our asses and pointing fingers at us for this."

MARCH 27TH, 2019, 2 A.M.

I feel a tap on my shoulder and open my eyes, seeing blurry lights in front of me. I rub my eyes and realize that I'm back in The Community's underground garage.

"We're here," Max says as he unlocks the doors and takes the keys out of the ignition.

I unbuckle myself and get out, adjusting my eyes to the bright lights of the parking lot. I am so thankful to be back. I stretch and grab my bag from the backseat. "Man, I can't wait to lay down," I say as we walk toward the elevator.

"I can tell you've had a long flight."

"Yeah. I know this will hurt in the morning," I say with a yawn. "I should message Morgana that I'm here. I really don't want to wake her up though."

"Well, you can stay at my place for the night. I promise not to wake you up in the morning."

"That sounds amazing. As long as I can lay down somewhere I'll be fine. I'm exhausted."

APRIL 20TH, 2019

I still can't believe I'm actually living in Max's apartment. When I got back from Mexico, this was the surprise, and I'm so happy that was it. I'm able to do this because our relationship has strengthened even more. Even though I lived like two floors down in the apartment, it's still allowing us to be closer.

The news of us living together spread really fast over these past few weeks and it may have been from confiding in Morgana, telling her about everything that's been going on with me. But who really knows if that was it?

Also, rumor has it that Sabrina, the meanest witch on the planet who did have a crush on Max, is devastated to the point of wanting to leave The Community, which I find pretty drastic—but then again, she is a horrible person and I'd rather have her gone.

Either way, drama aside, Max and I are really happy. Every night we have conversations about all kinds of things that I can't even imagine and, of course, there's more intimacy we both really enjoy. We've also been going out a lot more to alleviate some of the overall tension that's been occurring in Westwood itself with the first murder. So, of course, both of us are cautious.

"Oh, shit," Max says, while typing on his computer.

"What's going on?" I ask.

"Come look at this." He gestures me to his computer. I walk over and see an article from the local news.

"There's another murder reported in frat close by," he says with a sigh. "This isn't good at all."

I briefly skim the article while Max reads ahead. "It says that the victim died from the same method of suffocation with scratches along the back and across the chest. Same as the last one."

I meet his gaze. "Do you think ATX would say anything?" ATX is one of the hate groups disguised as a Christian frat that is adamant on trying to out us.

"I wouldn't be surprised. They've been trying to expose us for a while, so it's only a matter of time before we'd have to directly defend ourselves."

"Can't Leo find a way to see into the past and future to figure out who's behind this?"

He shakes his head. "There's some type of block that neither Leo nor Akasha can see who's behind this."

This isn't good at all.

MAY 12TH, 2019

The Community has been a mess since Max suddenly disappeared. We've all been trying to figure where he could've possibly went. And the worst part is, we can't even track a potential location given this mysterious block hindering our abilities. We're pretty much left to using the non-magical means of searching for him, which haven't been that great either. I've been worried so much. As every night passes, I fear the worst has happened, leading to a lot of sleepless nights. How am I supposed to balance this with class assignments?

I definitely need a break.

'"Hey, wanna see something cool?" Morgana says as we head down the trail to the botanical gardens. We always come here to just relax and meditate from school.

"Sure." I keep my gaze on the ground, making sure I don't step on loose rocks like last time. Ended up taking a pretty nasty fall. I still have a scar on my knee because I still love wearing shorts in March. Hey, it's spring in Los Angeles. I might as well embrace the weather!

We finally arrive at our favorite spot right next to an oak tree. It's known as the make out spot since it's hidden behind thick bushes, with a circular bench right underneath an old oak tree. I've been here a couple times with Max but today it's just a chill hangout with Morgana.

I place my backpack on the ground and find a comfortable spot on the bench.

Meanwhile, Morgana takes out an old spell book she found in The Community's library. She pulls out the book, its red leather faded into a light brown. Dust is still caked it all over, yet if one looks closely, they can see the triple moon pattern that had been etched in it long ago. I am still surprised this book remains intact.

"What are you doing?" I whisper while eyeing the book.

"I am gonna show you something cool."

"You know we're not supposed to out in public right?" I ask.

She shrugs. "Too late. I've been dying to try this spell out. I needed to be in nature to do it so we're in the perfect place," she says while flipping through the pages. I swear those pages will probably fall apart any minute.

"Ah, here it is." She opens the book completely then reaches into her backpack and pulls out her wand.

"Wait. I thought you said you weren't the *Harry Potter* witch," I say with a grin.

"Haha, very funny. I've always had one but just didn't have a purpose in using it all the time. I only use it when I want to invite a spirit in a spell, which you haven't seen me do before."

"Well, you probably shouldn't do spells here considering that we're technically in a public setting!" I say, stressing out.

"Relax. Here, let me show you how cool this wand is then decide if you want to see even more coolness that I can invoke," she says while handing it to me. I honestly expected it to look like my *Harry Potter* wand, you know, a thin long stick carved with a wooden handle.

This one was beautiful. It's so simplistic. I expected it to be covered in crystals of some sort but it's just a simple branch instead.

"Okay, so here's the cool part." Morgana lifts her wand while staring at the oak tree. I still wonder what she's gonna do. "You see this tree here?" she asks while turning to me. I nod. "Well, I am gonna make him talk."

"That's ridiculous," I say while taking a look behind me, making sure no one is around to see what she's about to do. "You're willing to risk exposing your powers while you try to talk to a tree?"

"It's not just a tree!" she exclaims. "It's the Greenman who is the nature deity in Wicca/Witchcraft. He's present in all living things but particularly plants. I'm hoping to call him into our world to see if we can find your missing boyfriend. So I am gonna do an invocation spell using my wand to invite the Greenman," Morgana explains as she looks down at the spell book one last time.

"Alright. Let's look at this," I say while sitting down on a nearby rock instead, giving her and myself space in case anything happens.

"Okay here it goes," she says while turning around. She faces the tree, wand poised in her hand.

"I call to the Greenman who resides in the north
I am the daughter of earth, who summon you forth
From caves and forests, from fields & their flowers

Bring abundance & joy in this sacred hour
Greenman who governs the love & the rain
Come from the west & push away pain
With each movement I make & breath that I take
Bring blessings, abundance & gain."

And with those last few words, she waves her wand in a diagonal hand motion. Suddenly, there is a loud crack, like a firework. As I gaze at the tree, I begin to see the bark… morph. It begins cracking, shifting the ridges in the bark into a shape. As the bark begins to morph, it lights up with a gentle orange glow. Now I can see an outline of a man's face, with the bark serving as makeshift wrinkles.

It's the Greenman.

"You dare summon me, puny human?" he barks at Morgana. Both of us are startled for a moment, yet Morgana is quick to respond to the Greenman in the most Morgana-like way possible

"Well, you didn't have to accept the invitation! I could have easily used my athame to command you, but I thought being nice would pay off."

"Ha! That athame would've done nothing. I am only summoned when there's a real problem or when witches like you decide to test their so called 'magical skills.'"

I can see the look of anger on his face. He reminds me of a grumpy old man "So, you called me and now I am here.

For what purpose do you summon me to this sad excuse of a garden?"

"My friend and I," she says while gesturing to me, "are trying to figure out what happened to her boyfriend. He's been missing for two weeks, yet we can't seem to figure out how or why he suddenly went missing."

"So you invoked me to somehow find some stranger of yours because one of you can't live without him?" he asks sarcastically. He gazes at me, his tree-bark-shaped eyes look me up and down from head to toe. "I can just smell the roses of a love spell on one of you. It's wretched."

"Well, I am not under a spell, but I do love him," I reply.

The Greenman rolled his eyes. "You mortals are so weak. You all would do anything for love. Luckily for me, I have never encountered love… would've been nice to have." He has a brief look of sadness before looking back up to Morgana and me.

"What I can tell you both is that forces beyond your control have taken the boy. He is somewhere out in this world that prevents me from seeing him. My guess is that evil forces have taken hold of him." He looks out into the distance. "Forces that desire destruction… and death."

We both look at each other. This is *not* good.

"You two, daughters of the goddess and Gaia, need to be careful. Darkness is rising. And you mortals are the key."

Suddenly, his orange glow begins to fade, the tree bark begins to morph back.

"Wait, no!" I exclaim as he begins to fade away.

"Key to what?" Morgana asks.

"Life," he whispers. The orange glow is gone. The tree is back to normal.

Now it's just us, with some vague message: *We're the key to life.*

CHAPTER 8

MAY 20ᵀᴴ, 2019

Cleaning the apartment on Saturdays is always a drag. It's even harder now given that I honestly don't have the motivation to do it. Even though it's just me in our apartment now, dishes still pile up, with some of them having been there since last week.

Usually, I just blast music with my headphones and start cleaning right away. I'd be preoccupied with something in the kitchen, usually earlier in the morning before Max gets up, then all of a sudden he'd come out of nowhere, wrapping me in his warm embrace.

He used to make cleaning not so depressing.

It used to be fun, romantic even.

I remembered the first time cleaning was romantic:

I was woken up by the sunshine from the window in my bedroom. The tiny slit through the curtains reminded me of the wonders being a morning person gave. Although Max was not a morning person, he managed to sleep beside me.

I tried not to wake him up as I gently turned myself toward him. I stroked his blond hair softly, admiring the man next to me. "I love when you do that."

I smiled. "You don't know how much I enjoy doing it."

He opens those powerful gray eyes. Those eyes have always made me weak.

He reaches over, stroking a strand of hair away from my face. "Morning, Beautiful."

I grin. "Morning, bae."

He pulls the cover off himself and leans over, his lips meeting mine.

I am blissed out, enjoying every moment of this, the movement of his lips against mine, my desire going through the roof.

He deepens the kiss, giving me signs he wants more.

And so do I.

I throw off the covers, wanting the feel of his body against mine.

His shirt disappears, followed by mine.

It's just the two us, embracing one another, enjoying the passion flowing through our veins.

I loved the remainder of that beautiful memory, but my mind is brought back to the present as I look at the calendar. It's been weeks and we still haven't made progress on finding him. I'm ready to just accept the worst. Morgana keeps assuring me that he'll either show up or we'll find him again this weekend on our search, but the chances of finding him have become slimmer with each passing day.

It'd be so easy to file a missing person's report, but since this happened more than likely because of The Dark Shadows, no one would believe us. Leo still hasn't had any luck in trying to find him either.

It just doesn't make any sense.

So after another restless night, I got up around 4 a.m. and decided to start cleaning. I stare at the pile of dishes, trying to somehow get the motivation to clean them, knowing damn well I don't want to. I go back on my phone, intending to find the perfect EDM song to drown out my thoughts. The beats make my body move, side to side, loving the soothing voice and upbeat pace, the piano mixed with EDM beats. It's the perfect temporary lift-me-up song.

After about what feels like an hour, all the dishes are done. Now it's time for the living room. Pretty soon the entire kitchen and living room are spotless. As I put away all the cleaning supplies, letting my EDM music flow through me, I don't know what else I can do. I check the clock on my phone: 6 a.m.

Damn.

I am wide awake this early. But I have no idea what else to do. But my stomach is begging me to cook. After making a tofu scramble, I turn on the TV to be greeted by the early news. Nothing but death, averse political policies, big corporations trying to limit holistic healing, and some drunk who made a potato gun using 3D printing. It's the usual, boring headlines that only make me worry more about the state of our planet.

Even though I am in no mood whatsoever to read about the dynamic of marriage for my psychology class, I decide I might as well study since I do not want to fail the second exam like I did with the first. I find it ironic that I have to read about love and relationships yet mine is in jeopardy since Max might already be dead.

I pick up my backpack lying next to the coffee table and pull out the intimate relationships textbook, flipping to the marriage section. All of my flashcards are in a jumbled mess, with a few falling to the floor. I try to recall a few terms: interdependence, desire, mutuality.

Yeah, no. This isn't happening.

I stare out the window, greeted by cloudy weather with a chance later on that it'll rain. I might as well step out on the balcony before it rains, just to get some fresh air. I walk back to the bedroom and grab my stress relief box, take my vape pen, and head out to the balcony, the morning dark and gloomy. Although my thoughts are slightly calmed down, I realize just how bad this might be. I usually try to mediate or somehow assure myself he's safe. But I've reached a point where even that is not attainable.

I stare out at the street, holding the vape pen in my hand, wishing that I could find some sort of happiness in this time of stress galore. I still don't understand how I'm supposed to discover my other abilities of air and spirit when I am confined to this misery of emotions. What makes this worse is the tension I feel knowing there's a war happening when the next solar eclipse happens. Quetzal had warned me during my training.

> As I look out my window, I see the full moon shining over the desert like a beacon in the darkness. I've always love astronomy and anything related to it and especially the moon, having seen it rise and set every dusk to dawn. Suddenly, I hear Quetzal knock on the door.
>
> "Just wanted to check in, Mija." He sees me glancing out the window admiring the full moon.
>
> "Did you know la luna is tied to many Aztec legends?" Quetzal asks while we both look out the window.
>
> "I didn't. But I'd love to know more."
>
> "Well, in Aztec mythology, the moon was seen as an omen given its appearance at night, a time synonymous with

death and darkness. It had the ability to predict wars, famine, and death. It's also said that thousands of years ago, there would be a time in which the sun and moon will meet, creating a beautiful sight of light and dark, but that meeting would be the symbol of darkness reigning upon the earth."

"*That meeting is a solar eclipse. right?*"

He nods. "I fear that this eclipse will happen very soon. And when it does, it'll cause a war between the light and the dark."

"*How soon will it happen?*"

He shrugs. "My prediction is that'll happen in summer given the excitement the world is feeling with the upcoming solar eclipse."

"*Wait, isn't the moon going to be the closest it's ever been for a solar eclipse?" I look away from the full moon and meet his gaze.*

"*Brace for the war, child," he replies.*

How can I prepare for this when I can't even manage to control my emotions? My depression and anxiety overwhelm me, like a blanket that promises warmth yet fills me with dread and despair. It gives me so much false hope, yet some form of hope is better than none. Suddenly, I hear a voice in the back of my mind. *Look across.*

I look across the street and notice someone walking up a side street that leads straight The Community. I run inside and grab my glasses, seeing the blurry figure turn clear as day. I know that blond hair, that body, the dark shirt and jeans outfit.

"Max?"

He's back.

MAY 29TH, 2019
10 a.m.

"Where were you last night?" I ask Max as we washed the dishes. We finally have a Friday off from classes, yet we still have to do chores like this. I remember when this used to be fun, romantic even. I thought that having Max back in my life would make things better again; would end those horrible lonely nights, would bring back that passion we used to have.

Turns out I was wrong.

He's been so cold and distant ever since he returned from his mysterious absence. It's as if he's under a spell; a spell in which anger and frustration are his only two emotions. We can't seem to ever be happy. I am worried sick, and I fear the worst. But I don't think it's because of that. I just feel that something is… *off*. Honestly, I think he's cheating. And I have to find out for sure.

"I was out," replies Max.

"Doing what?" I ask.

"Things," he says the while rinsing the last dish. Right as he turns around to walk away, I break.

"It's a girl, isn't it?" I ask.

Max stops mid-stride "You think I'm cheating?"

I nod. "You've been the shittiest boyfriend ever since you got back. You pretty much ignore me, won't talk to me for days, even though we live in the same apartment. You're out late for days on end come back reeking of alcohol and weed. It's like you're becoming some stranger. I hate this new you."

There is silence between us. But I still don't think he got the message. "Yeah, I party with Harden's friends and we do go crazy. I just have to, you know, relax. I think I want to explore more of the party culture. And this whole relationship thing just fell for a few, but I'll work on it okay, I promise."

"Wait, who the hell is Harden?"

"He's a friend."

I still don't believe him. I shake my head and finish the rest of the dishes.

7 p.m.

"I don't know what's going on with him, but I am not staying there." I place my backpack on my bed, full of some of my stuff from his apartment.

"Girl, you should just move back in with me. It sucks to see you going through this." Morgana sits down at her desk.

"I just don't know what happened to him when he was gone. He's completely neglected the entire Community and now parties in God knows which one of the frats."

"I never thought he'd end up being this way with you, especially in your very first relationship," she says sympathetically.

"Exactly!" I exclaim. "It's frustrating as hell. I know for a fact that the Max who came back is a totally different person than the Max I knew. Instead of being with me, he's prioritizing partying with some dude name Harden."

"Harden?" Morgana asks.

"Yeah. Do you know who he is?" I say ask.

She nods. "I mean the Harden I know about is like the president of ATX but I could be wrong."

"No. There's no way it's that guy."

"Well, I don't know if you'd asked before but does he say where these parties are at?"

"Not really. One time, he said it was somewhere on Kelton, which again is very vague."

"No. It's not vague at all." Morgana reaches for her phone and scrolls through it. Her eyes widen. "This isn't good at all."

"Why?"

She meets my gaze. "ATX is on Kelton. And you mentioned the name Harden, so..."

"He's partying with them after all. He must be there all of the time because I hardly ever see him."

"Wait, didn't you mention something about Harden and Madison before?" she asks.

I shake my head. "I don't think so?" I've ignored everything about her since the incident.

"Yeah. I could've sworn you said she was dating someone named Harden."

Oh, shit. "I wouldn't be surprised if she's dating him. It would make sense though."

"So, Madison, who's the spawn of the devil, is dating Harden who's..."

"Partying with Max," I say. We're silent for a moment in shock as we piece together the puzzle.

"You need to get out of his apartment. Who knows what's going on with him."

MAY 30TH, 2019
12 p.m.

I get back into his apartment to move all of my stuff back to apartment with Morgana. I empty out all of my clothes from the dresser that I shared with him and make one last stop to the bathroom to get my toiletries out of the way. As I pack my bag, I notice something in the trash can.

That's when things click.

I was right.

We hadn't done that in months but now, I know. It probably happened in this room, in the same bed.

No.

I feel the knot in my stomach, making me nauseated as hell. I get everything that I've packed up, and I leave. I run out of his apartment up the stairs to the third floor. I dump all my stuff on the floor and sit on my bed and begin full on sobbing. I hear the bathroom door open.

"Girl, I'm here. It's okay." Morgana hugs me, letting my cry.

"I found out he's cheating," I say in between sniffles. "Why does this have to happen to me?" I ask even though I don't expect an answer.

"I don't know, girl. It's hard but you know staying here with me is a lot better than staying with him."

"I know," I reply.

10 p.m.

Max finally schedules a meeting for The Community after weeks without one. I seriously don't want to go but I do have to hear what's been going on given the murders and protecting ourselves. It's horrible having to sit through it now knowing that Max is an ass. As I sit through almost an hour of him updating us on the latest news, I keep praying for this to end. I hate that there's so much important information I need to know. Otherwise, I would've left a long time ago. He's talking about something with The Council when he suddenly pauses and reaches for his phone, quickly speaking softly to whoever it is so we can't hear, yet I manage to hear the last few lines.

"Hey, Violet. Yeah, of course."

Violet? Who the hell is Violet?

"Okay, gotta go, bye." He hangs up the phone. "Alright, everyone, The Community meeting is over. You all can head back to your rooms."

As soon as everyone is out of the meeting room, I remain behind, staring at the floor then meeting his gaze.

"Hey, Cur." He walks closer, reaching for my hand.

"Don't even dare!" I pull it away from him, taking a step back.

"Wow, someone's in a bad mood," he replies.

"It's her, isn't it?" I ask

"What?"

"Violet," I say, meeting his gray eyes. Those eyes are usually my weakness, but now they are anger provoking.

"What about her?"

"I am not a dumbass. I saw the condom in the bathroom."

His face pales.

I shake my head, holding back the urge to break down.

"Look, I can explain—"

"No!" I yell. "You piece of shit." I feel a tear roll down my cheek. "You've been such an asshole ever since you got back. You hardly ever talk to me, always blaming me for every little thing that goes wrong. You're always saying you'll be back on Friday nights but then you don't show up until early as hell on Sunday morning, stinking of alcohol and here I am worrying something happened to you. And you still expect us to share the same bed knowing that you screwed someone random chick?"

"Cur, it won't happen again. I promise."

"That's your response?" I can't stand looking at him and begin to sob tears of anger and frustration. I speed walk out of the room, wiping the tears away.

"Cur, wait!" he says in the distance.

"Go enjoy your other woman," I exclaim while walking toward the stairwell. I briefly turn around and meet his gaze. "Better yet, go missing for another three weeks but this time don't come back!"

I run down the stairs, holding onto the guardrail to make sure I don't fall. I feel the pavement under my feet, hear my footsteps echo. I reached into my jeans pocket, thankful to feel the metal of my car keys against my thigh. I run faster now out onto the street. I am so thankful that these streets are empty at 11 p.m.

I don't know where I'm heading but I'm hoping it's far away from here as possible. My car is down the road. *Yes!* I parked it in kind of a secluded spot since I was planning to leave for Joshua Tree tomorrow morning because I need to get away from all of this. I am pretty sure I have some stuff packed but I can pick up the rest of it along the way. I turned on Kelton Avenue, feeling the adrenaline in my veins. I can hear Max in the distance, but he's lost now.

I find my car, open the door and put the keys in the ignition. The car rumbles to life, and I put it in drive. I head toward the freeway. I get on the 405 and head north for a few miles. I pull over for gas and turn off my phone. Luckily, there's a nearby 7-Eleven so I walk in and notice the man behind the register.

I ask him for an old-fashioned map. I remember using those in high school, when I finally got my driver's license and I wanted to get away from everyone and everything, I would get an old-fashioned map so I could turn off my phone and live in the moment.

"Going off the grid, huh?" The man behind the register asks, his thick Spanish accent kind of making it a little difficult to understand.

"Yep. I'm heading to Joshua Tree for a weekend," I reply.

"Ah," he says while he reaches under the counter and pulls out a map. "Here's the perfect map. Up-to-date and accurate. From here, you'd want to hit the 210 so you're gonna have to take multiple freeways. Best bet is to hit the 10 but—"

"Thank you," I say as I hand the man money for that, a pack of waters, basic toiletries, and a phone charger.

I check my Airbnb notification for tomorrow morning. Hopefully, they'll let me come in a few hours earlier; maybe even tonight if I'm lucky but I doubt that they'd have it ready by then. Either way, I don't care. I just want to get away from all of this. I get back in my car and head back on the freeway, listening to my *Avicii CD*.

I love his music. He can make the shittiest breakup of all time feel less devastating. I can't take all of this craziness anymore. An impending war happening in a few months, Max leaving mysteriously and coming back three weeks later, creating hell all over the place, then I'm trying to balance that while trying to be a normal college student. Oh, and did I mention I ended up failing a class too? It's all just too overwhelming.

Yet, somehow, I'm supposed to manage this even though I have to figure out why I am important in this upcoming war. This whole situation is so overwhelming. And I didn't think I'd ever fall in love either. I always thought it was part of movies and books—basically fiction. My psychology class is so true though. They say that intimate relationship problems can cause you to either go really crazy or can hurt you the most.

That's definitely true in my life.

Max has been causing me so many issues. He just came back a totally different person, but I just wonder what happened when he left. He doesn't talk about it all. Like I said before, it's as if he's under a spell of some sort. I wish I could have somebody fix him with another spell, but it seems like this is not gonna happen. I just hate that these past few weeks all I can think about is Max and how he's treated me.

And yeah, I probably don't know this Violet chick but, trust me, I hate her most out of everyone. I hate her. I hate math. I hate everything! I get tired of thinking, so I put the radio on since my Avicii CD is finally done. As I put the radio on, I hear my other favorite artists. I notice there are no more city lights to comfort me along this drive. For a moment, I am frightened because everything is dark, but I am so thankful that there is also a full moon providing me with abundant light to continue on this long drive. I roll down my window and feel the breeze of the cold night air.

I'm honestly thankful that it's almost June because this breeze feels amazing. The radio keeps playing and I just tune it out. It gives me a sense of calm otherwise had everything been completely silent, I probably would've freaked out. I missed this feeling of driving on my own; going to wherever I want to be able to escape from everything. Yeah, I'm a little worried that nobody knows where I'm at, but that's also kind of the beauty of it.

As I pass a sign that says *Needles, CA*. I pull over to the side of the road and turn on my phone and go back onto my Airbnb and notification. I call the person in charge of my Airbnb, letting them know that I encountered an emergency and I would love to stay the night before. Even though it's probably around 11 p.m., she's very respectful and I am able to stay at the place now.

And yes, I'm tired of looking at the old-fashioned map so I put the Airbnb address into my navigation. I also notice about six missed calls, ten text messages from who knows who, five voicemails, and a whole bunch of social media notifications.

But I don't answer any of them.

I head off on the road, admiring the beauty yet also the dark aspects of nature. I can't believe it's almost midnight and I'm driving to the desert. I am almost to Joshua Tree, but I still can't believe I did this. If my parents ever knew I was doing this, they would call me a crazy ass and tell me that I'll probably get captured by the night burglar or who knows what. This is therapeutic to me; this is how I can relax from all this shit that's been going on. So, I'm going to continue on this drive although I probably will need gas soon.

This journey is amazing, and I am excited to see what the desert will look like in the morning although I am really tired now. I still have another hour to go. As I think about this, I keep a mental note in the back of my mind.

You are worthy of it. You are worthy of this journey, and you are worthy of love and care. Don't let Max mess things up, don't doubt yourself, and yes, let yourself cry.

1 a.m.

JOSHUA TREE

The Airbnb is a small guest house just right outside the main town in Joshua Tree. It's beautiful but I'm slightly scared since I'm hearing coyotes howl. The only source of light is the partially full moon, and I really want to get inside the house. I put the code in the lock keypad and it opens with a *click*. I rush inside, close the door, and turn on the lights.

It's a beautiful guest house with a small kitchen area with makeshift a new table and the other room has a bed, a couch, and a small bathroom. I honestly don't care about my daily routine as I am so tired and also quite frightened by the coyotes, so I leave the kitchen light on, remove my shirt and pants, and climb into bed. I can't wait to see what will happen tomorrow.

MEANWHILE BACK IN WESTWOOD…

"What happened to her?" Morgana says while pounding on Max's door. "What did you do to her?"

He opens the door, seeing Morgana's furious gaze. "Cur's been gone for hours, and I can't get a hold of her."

"Look, it's hard to explain, okay? I know I haven't been the best boyfriend to her but—"

''What did you do to her?" She enunciates each word with a menacing attitude.

"I messed up. I started hanging out with Harden and I slept with one of his friends."

"Wow." She shakes her head. "You piece of shit! How could you do this to her?"

"I don't know. I don't know what's making me do this." Max leans against the wall, gripping his face with his hands. "This isn't me. It's like someone else's living in my body. It doesn't seem right to me, but something just keeps calling me to Harden and his group of horrible frat guys. I don't know what it is. Cur ended up finding the condom in the bathroom. She confronted me about it about an hour ago and we got into a fight. She took off to God knows where. I tried calling her but she's not answering me either."

"I swear, if she doesn't come back alive, I will kill you," Morgana says, anger livid in her voice. "You know that she is struggling with so many things; you know she's under a lot of pressure with so many other aspects of her life. You know that doing this to her might push her over the edge. With her past of mental health issues, it's concerning on so many levels. So I pray to the Goddess that she comes out of this alive."

"I've been trying to track her on Snapchat but seems like she's off the grid."

"Well, keep trying. It's unfortunate I can't use my magic to find her, otherwise I would. God dammit, Max!" She storms off down the hallway. **Back in Joshua Tree...**

> *I am lying down by a pool, feeling the sun's heat against my skin. It feels so soothing, warm. Comforting even. I don't want this to end. Ever. I reach over my chair and grab the tropical smoothie brought to me by the butlers serving everyone else. This is the type of desert tropical vacation I had in mind.*
>
> *I decide it's time for a nice dip in the pool. I walk over to the stairs, grab onto the rail, and gently walk into the pool. The coolness of the water soothes me. Makes me feel like home. I could stay here forever. Suddenly, I see something in the water. Its eyes stare back at me. This is not human. It's an…*
>
> Alligator.

I wake up, startled as hell. I realized that I am no longer at a pool, but instead, I am lying face down on a pillow in an unfamiliar house. *That was all a dream.* I actually made it to Joshua Tree and this unfamiliar house is my Airbnb place for the next week.

And this place needs AC *now*.

I get up from the bed and look around for the thermostat. After a few moments, I find it next to the blinds. I turn the thermostat down to 70 and I draw the blinds open, the sun scorching its way through. This little house is *hot*. I love the heat though; it keeps me alive and gives me a reason to stay on this planet. It's amazing that Mother Nature can have such a profound effect on me.

I get up and I notice my phone sitting on the bed table. It's already 8 a.m. Oh, man, I should probably message everyone back home. Then again, I don't want Max to come find me. I'll message Morgana. I open Snapchat and reply to her messages, telling her that I'm safe and sound. That's when I get a phone call from her.

"Girl, are you okay? Max told me everything that happened between you two last night. I wanted to call to make sure that you made it there alive and didn't die en route."

"Yes, I am fine. Although it was scary hearing the coyotes at 1 a.m., I managed to get here. I'm gonna be staying these next two nights. I figured I needed to get away from everything."

Especially since Max pushed me over the edge.

"I was worried sick about you last night and you should've at least messaged me halfway through, you know?"

"I understand," I reply. "I just didn't want to get back on the grid because I didn't want to have to think about Max. I didn't want to be tempted to message him or even have him find me and come drive out here. I don't want to be in his life anymore, and I don't want him in my life either if he's still this complete mess. He can go back with Violet or whatever her name is. I don't want to be associated with him anymore."

"He's messing around with Violet? Of all people, he would go with her?"

"Yeah. Do you know her?"

"She's definitely part of ATX. I've had a few encounters with her during her religion tirade on campus. She's the meanest bitch I've ever encountered. She kept yelling out that I was a witch and even walked over to the other people chilling on Janss Steps and warned them that I'm an evil satanic witch. That same day, she tried following me back to the dorms like a stalker. I eventually confronted her, cussed her out, and scared her ass away with my athame."

"Holy shit. Why didn't you tell me?"

"It happened before we met. I couldn't really tell anyone about this so I've always kept it hidden. It was in the back of my mind for the longest time but when we found out about this whole thing with Max, her name just brought up the memory. I'll never forget that bitch."

Dear God. And Max is messing with her of all people.

"Yeah," I reply. "Hey, I'd rather not talk about that anymore. I don't know. Something doesn't seem right about this whole situation. He would *never* do this."

"I think something's fishy about this too. I think I might have Leo take a look and see what's going on with Max."

"Thanks. And I have some events scheduled for this week like meditation and Reiki energy healing so I'm going to be kind of busy. I'll message you during the week and will be back on Friday night or afternoon depending on traffic. Thanks for checking in."

"No problem, girl. Have fun. Be safe. Love you lots."

"Love you too," I say as I hang up the call.

MAY 30TH, 2019, JOSHUA TREE, 8 P.M.

Finally, the sun set. The temperature outside, although still hot as hell, is slightly cooler than during the day. I pack my backpack with my binoculars, a sweater, water bottle, phone battery pack, and a map. I'll be driving for about thirty minutes into the park, but it'll be totally worth it. I head on the dirt road then got on the main highway toward the park. Minutes pass as I take in the scenery.

The beautiful Joshua trees look like old wise men with long beards. It's as if they have a collective message, one that I seek to find out as soon as I find a place to decently camp out despite just having a blanket and no tent. I continue on the road and I notice the welcome sign fly past me. I'm in.

I start to scout for the perfect rock or spot in general. Minutes pass. Then I see the perfect spot. I pull to the side of the main road and head down the dirt side road, seeing a plethora of Joshua trees and rocks. The sky is turning into a blue and purple hue. I decide it's right to stop the car. I park on the dirt road and pop the trunk. I grab my backpack and emergency blanket, hoping none of the insects decide to snack on my legs. Not my fault I drove here in shorts.

At least I was smart enough to pack hiking boots. I walk for a few minutes, just taking in the beauty of the sunset, seeing how the sky begins to darken. That's when I start to see the stars. Large orbs of different-colored lights span out through the sky. I never knew stars could actually have a color aside from white. That's the default in LA but here you get to see *everything.* It's mesmerizing.

As I keep walking, I notice a large flat rock right in between two Joshua trees. They're bent over the spot, as if guarding it. This is the perfect. I place my blanket on it and step onto it. It's a fairly large rock, about the size a dining room table but not that thick where I would need to jump up. I just had to lift my short ass up a little more than usual but it's totally worth it.

Once I am on the rock, I place my backpack beside me, taking out my binoculars, camera, and water bottle. I am going to take a few pictures, look at the stars for a few moments to ground myself, then I will get into contact zone. Usually, I have my sound bowl, sage, and all that, but I didn't have time to get them given the fact I just drove off haphazardly. So, I am going to make do without them. We'll manage somehow.

I take a few pictures of the park, the sky giving an amazing background, take my binoculars and look at the bright orbs in the sky, then take a drink of water. It's beautiful out here but damn, it's hot even at night. A few moments pass. I think it's time to place all my crap away and just… be.

Now's the perfect time to see if I can access the last earth element: air. Quetzal said I have the ability to tap into it but I still don't know how. Plus, I need answers to what's been going on with Max. I need some guidance. First, I need to get grounded. I sit cross-legged. I breathe in a few times, making sure to have equal breaths in and out. In for five, hold, out for five. Repeating this path over and over again. I notice how the rock feels against my legs, its strong yet smooth surface. How it supports me between these two Joshua Trees. My mind is quiet. It's not thinking about anything. Just being here in the moment.

That's when I feel it. That familiar warmth I feel while channeling traveling from my feet upward. Suddenly, I start to hear a voice in the back of my head. It's guiding me to invoke Quetzalcoatl, the Aztec god of wisdom, courage, and life, something I have never done before.

> *I invoke Quetzalcoatl, god of wisdom, of life. Be with me in this sacred hour of strife So that I may gain insight On the reason for my fright. Help me understand why I think there may be a lie hiding behind the shadows. Quetzal, guide me, lead me, help me.*

I chant over and over, letting the words come to me freely.

Suddenly, I feel a soft feather stroking my arm. I open my eyes and I see a green snake, with red and green feathers wrapped around its head, slithering down my arm. I should be scared seeing this, should be freaking out and throwing the snake on the ground.

But I'm not.

It slithers down my legs and off the rock onto the ground a few feet away. It turns around, revealing bright green eyes. It hisses at me, but I don't move an inch. It's somehow a welcoming presence. It wraps itself into a ball and begins to emit green smoke. The smoke figure starts to light up, with neon green light surrounding it.

It forms into a man but no ordinary man. Quetzalcoatl has a green feathered headpiece with feathers reaching two feet long. He's wearing a green tunic from the waist down, his body covered in green armor, while his neck has a green amulet. His figure solidifies completely, revealing bright green eyes like those of a snake.

"You summon me, child?"

I nod and meet his gaze. "I am in need of guidance. I feel that there is a something hidden that no one, not even I, is capable of seeing. I feel that darkness has overtaken the one person I love the most." I stare at the ground, silent for a moment. "I don't want to lose him." A tear rolls down my cheek.

"There is darkness in the boy you love. But neither you nor your friends can banish it." He looks out toward the vast desert. "That darkness comes from the underworld, a place I have no control over. There is one thing you can do." He looks at me, his eyes feel like they're staring right through me. "You can keep the darkness from completely taking over him through memory."

"Memory?" I ask. "What does that mean?"

"Remind him of the times when everything was positive, when there was love and happiness. It will keep the boy grounded."

I nod, taking in this information, trying to remember some of the many memories I had with Max before his disappearance, but right away, Quetzalcoatl brings me back to reality. "And dear child, you must practice using your powers. Try out here in the beauty of this desert." He gestures to the wide-open space with the occasional Joshua tree in the distance.

"I don't know if I can use my powers. I managed to do it before but barely being able to do little things lighting a candle won't help me save humanity."

"You can save humanity with your powers but you have to believe in yourself. You have to trust me and yourself, child."

I nod, glancing at the palms of my hands. I look up, meeting his gaze.

"You can do this. I and all of the gods above will be watching over you," he replies with his hands reaching toward the sky. He gazes up at the stars, the band of the Milky Way shining bright against the sky. He looks back at me. "I will be leaving now. Embrace your gifts, child. You are capable of so much. Keep the darkness out of the boy with memory. And prepare." He looks off into the distance once more. "For the great war."

And with that, Quetzalcoatl disappeared in a blink of an eye.

I can't keep doubting my powers any longer. I used them back with Quetzal and have to use them know. I have the power of controlling the earth elements. And I will use them to fight in the war.

I walk over to a nearby Joshua tree. I place my hand over it, with no intention of reviving it. I imagine my hands holding spheres of fire, ready to burn the poor thing in order to make room for new life. I imagine my palms glowing brighter with fire. Suddenly, I feel that intense warmth like I did with the candle. Both of my palms start to glow bright orange, with tendrils of fire emanating from my body. I stand back a few feet. With the soles of my feet planted on the ground and my arms outstretched in front of me, I take a deep breath, bend my arms back as if I had a bat, and swing them forward. Fire shoots forth like a flame thrower, burning the tree.

It lights up immediately, covered in bright orange flames. It looks mesmerizing against the night sky. But I cannot look at it for much longer because it will catch someone's attention. I cup my hands together and close my eyes, feeling the night breeze cool my skin. I imagine that breeze extinguishing the flames. I place my hands out in front of me, concentrating on the wind, feeling it course through my veins down to the depths of my soul.

I start noticing the smell of incinerated tree when I place my hands in front of me in a pushing motion. The wind rushes past me, minimizing the flames slightly. Wind isn't going to do it either. I bend down and feel the dirt, becoming fully aware of the sand and dirt mixture.

Nope. I know what I need to do.

I walk over to my spot and pick up my water bottle. I open the cap and pour it over my left hand, followed by my right. I rub my palms together and look at the fire growing brighter. *This has to stop now.*

I stretch out my arms once more, thinking about the ocean, of the sound of the rain. Water flows from my hands in a thick stream, almost like a waterfall. All that's left is the sound of the water extinguishing the flames. The charred remnants of the tree begin to slowly fall, its ashes spread around it. But we're not done yet.

I walk toward the burned tree. I place my hands on it, not capable of feeling the painful heat. It feels warm, like feeling a fire from a distance. I grip the ashy stem. I channel everything I have, remembering how it looked before I burned it. It's green pointed top with the beard shape of dried leaves.

Give this tree life. I repeat it over and over like a mantra.

Suddenly, I feel it jerk. It twitches, as if an animal were crawling in it. As if it were *alive*. It begins to grow right before my eyes, sprouting upward. Although I can't see its greenness in the dark, I can still see it sprouting and coming back to life.

Fire, air, water, earth. My elements.

I hear Quetzalcoatl's voice in the back of my head. "You're missing one more."

I'll find it when the eclipse happens.

CHAPTER 9

BATTLE PREP—JUNE 1ST, 2019

The drive back from Joshua Tree is probably the hardest thing I have to do. I had an amazing time this week of yoga, journaling, and going out to see the stars. And I had spoken to Quetzalcoatl. Now I know what may be going on with Max and I was right: the darkness had gotten him. Or should I say the Dark Shadows. Honestly, same thing.

Something is wrong and now I have an idea why. I knew Max wouldn't be this much of an asshole. I pack everything in the trunk and head back inside, making sure I have all my things. I am going to miss this desert vacation, from seeing the stars to testing out my new skills. But I need to get back as soon as possible. The Community doesn't know what we need to do with this impending war. It's a few weeks away yet all we've been doing is just practicing our powers.

I didn't try to practice in the Spellcasting Room considering the fact that my powers are dangerous, especially the fire-casting skills. Plus, ever since my trip to Mexico, I never thought I had the power to fully control the elements. But this trip made me believe that I can.

I get in my car, turn the key in the ignition and drive off.

Luckily, it's about 5 a.m. so the sun hasn't even come up yet, but the warmth is still rampant but slightly cooler. It's going to be a long drive back to Westwood, but I have to head back. I just can't believe I had done something impulsive like this driving over here a day early. That's not like me at all. I usually plan things out beforehand, not just running away to forget about it. I just wonder why I had acted out like that today.

Wait.

Max. He's capable of manipulating emotion, thoughts.

Is he?

No. NO.

He can't be controlling mine. He said he could never read me, could never get into my thoughts as if there was a barrier of some sort.

What if the Dark Shadows removed that block? Oh, no.

I try to keep my focus on the long desert road ahead, but I am so tempted to call Morgana. Maybe this is the revelation Quetzal was trying to tell me. I glance out the window and start to notice more city life.

How long have I been driving? I check the clock on my dashboard: 6:30 a.m. Wow. Time does fly when you get lost in thought. As I glance at the road, I pick up my phone and quickly dial Morgana, hoping that she wouldn't mind me calling her. I hear the phone ring a few times, ready to just end the call when the ringing stops.

"Cur?" Morgana yawns. "You woke me up. What's up?"

"Girl, I am so sorry I called. I'm on my way back."

"Okay. Well, have fun wit—"

"I think I found out what's been going on with Max."

She's quiet for a few moments. I hear rustling. "What? How?"

"I ended up contacting Quetzalcoatl. Remember the Aztec serpent God I told you about?" I ask.

"Yeah, I think so."

"Well, he visited me in the desert and told me that The Dark Shadows have taken over Max."

"Wait, what? Really?" she asks.

"Yes. And honestly, do you think that I am *that* impulsive that I would just take off after that fight we got into?"

"Well, I did think it was off from what you usually do. I just thought it was because love drove you out there."

"No, girl. It wasn't love. You know Max's gift, right?"

She's quiet for a moment then I hear a loud sound from her. "Oh, my Goddess!" she exclaims as realization hits her. "Do you think he's really manipulating your thoughts? I thought he couldn't because of some block?"

"But that block could've been destroyed if the Dark Shadows are involved."

"Holy shit." I hear more rustling on her end. "It makes sense. I tried asking Leo to see if he can find something wrong, and he just couldn't understand why. He just said it was dark and murky."

"That makes full-proof sense. It's possible that Max's disappearance may have involved him being captured by them then released to affect me."

"But why though?" Morgana asks. "It makes no sense that the Dark Shadows would want you."

Or it does. Given my newfound abilities.

"I don't know why." *I have to tell them about my true powers soon.* "Hey, Morgana?"

"Yeah?" she asks.

"I found out what my true powers are. And I don't feel safe showing them around Max."

"What? No way!" she yells. "I am so happy for you!"

"Thanks, girl. But this is serious though. We can't let Max find out since he's under some type of evil influence. I need a place to practice back home. Somewhere safe but not The Community."

"Hmm." She goes quiet like she's lost in a thought for few moments. Meanwhile, I am trying to find a place too. "I might have an idea," she finally responds.

"What?" I ask.

"We can practice in an abandoned warehouse I know about. I used to meet with my coven there years ago. It's somewhere in The Valley but it's perfect."

"Well, I am on my way now. I'm thinking we can we meet there. Can you send me the address?"

"Yeah. Hold on." I hear rustling and noise for a few moments then I hear a ding from my phone. I glance and see a new message from Morgana, containing coordinates for the location. I put that into my navigation. ETA one hour.

"Awesome. It' about an hour away for me. Can you meet me there in an hour or so?"

"Yeah, girl, of course. You got to show me those powers. And I'll get there earlier to set up a protection spell."

"Great. Also bring something to rep the elements like fire, water, you know what I mean, right?" I ask her.

"Oh, yeah. I'll bring that. I'll see you in an hour, Cur."

"Thanks, girl. See ya." I hang up the phone, dreading the next hour of freeway to go.

8 a.m.

I arrive at the warehouse. It's in the middle of nowhere. Although The Valley is known to have desolate places, I was not expecting *this* desolate. It's the only warehouse for miles. I do hope no one decides to take a random trip to this abandoned place. I text Morgana, letting her know that I got here. The sun is finally shining. I love the warmth of it. I get closer to the fence encompassing the warehouse when I hear Morgana's voice.

"Cur."

I turn around.

The entirety of The Community, minus Max, stood behind her. Morgana carries a shoulder bag with her.

"Morgana, I thought you wouldn't tell—"

"Max has been an ass to all of us. So, he doesn't deserve to see what you're capable of. We've all been practicing in hiding ever since Max started being this pretentious asshole." She walks over to the fence, yanks on it, and tears off a huge chunk. It almost looks like a makeshift door. "This is where we practice now."

"I don't understand. I never knew about this."

"Because you were too close to Max. Hell, you lived with him up until a week ago. But once you called me this morning, we knew our intuitions were right."

"What, that he might be evil?"

She nods. "We all suspected some type of darkness took over him. But, of course, him owning the whole damn place, we couldn't just drop everything and leave. It would look suspicious. Luckily, he didn't come back last night so we're guessing he was at those parties again or something."

I nod. I feel the pain deep within me. I thought he loved me. But now I know Max really isn't Max. He's something... *evil*.

"So, Cur," Morgana says while stepping through the gate. "You got to tell us what you've been hiding. I know there's something profound within you, but you're scared to tell."

"I do. I can help us prepare for the war. And I can show you all what I am really capable of."

"Perfect." She turns toward The Community, "Everyone," she yells to them. "We're going to head inside and work on defensive spells as soon as Cur shows us her true powers."

She turns around and gestures me forward. I walk through the makeshift door, letting Morgana lead the way. We all walk toward the side entrance of the warehouse. We reach an old wooden door and Morgana places her hand in front of her. She begins to chant quietly: *"Intres licet dignis."*

The door opens with a loud squeak and she pushes it open farther. "Come on in." She gestures for me and The Community to enter. It's almost pitch black minus the little amount of sunlight making its way through small cracks in the ceiling.

Suddenly, I hear a loud click and a burst of bright light coming from behind me.

"Unfortunately, we don't have enough lighting, so we have to make do with this large lantern," she says while walking toward the middle of the warehouse and placing it on the floor, the white light creating a beacon. The warehouse looks almost empty aside from the random dummy doll in the center, a large book on the floor, and a workout mat.

"Nice place you got here, girl," I say while walking toward the doll, seeing a whole lotta marks on it. They clearly have been using it to help them.

"Thanks, Cur." She approaches me, handing me her bag. "Everything you asked for is in here. We really want to see what you can do."

I nod, opening the bag. I take out a water bottle, a tiny succulent, a candle, and a pack of incense cones. This is perfect.

"Alrighty," I say as I step away from the dummy and toward an empty corner of the warehouse. "Wait. Do you guys have something that you don't care about?"

"What do you mean?" Morgana asks.

"Do you have something to destroy?"

"We do." Will walks toward me carrying a wooden stick. "It was here for the longest time. Maybe you can do something with it," he says, handing me the stick.

"Yep. I'll do something with it." I place the stick about ten feet away from me and set up shop. I place the candle in front of me, the water bottle and succulent near me. I can feel everyone watching me, my body tensing, my heart beating slightly faster. I take a deep breath to relax my nerves. *I have to do this.* I close my eyes, holding my hands over the candle. I envision orange light emanating from my palms, lighting the candle.

I imagine the warmth of the candle being lit. That's when I feel it. That intense warmth. I open my eyes and see two small balls of fire. Everyone gasps but I continue to focus on my power. The orbs of fire get bigger in my palms and I place them closer to the candle. I place my right palm at the wick and within seconds, I hear the crackle and pop. I pull my hands away and see the candle fully ignited. *Perfect.*

"She can control fire?" someone shouts from The Community. Now, I own this place.

"We're not done yet," I say as I get up and eye the old piece of wood. I outstretch my right arm, imagining the fire being released from my palms. I feel the warmth and within seconds, a stream of fire emanates, burning the wood.

"Holy shit," Morgana yells. The fire quickly engulfed the wood, creating a bright orange glow.

"We need water!" someone shouts.

"I got it," I say while reaching down and opening the bottle of water. I pour it over my hands, rub my palms together, and stretch them in front of me. I feel the coolness of the water as it streams out of my hands, extinguishing the fire. I wipe my hands on my shorts and sit down by the succulent. I place my right palm over the candle flame and feel the warmth of the orange orb in my hand develop once more and set the succulent on fire, and extinguish it

This time, I place my hands over the succulent. I imagine it being lush and green. I imagine seeing fertile green lands. Within seconds, I can feel the warmth, but this isn't like the fire warmth. It's a gentle warmth that is always accompanied by sudden smell of pine trees. I look down and see the succulent begin to rise, shedding its charred petals into a new lush plant.

"Damn," someone yells from the crowd.

"I need one more thing." I walk over to the pack of incense cones, crouch, and place one not the floor. I light it with my palms and let the smoke rise upward. I stand, reaching my hand outward, feeling the warm tendrils move through my fingers. I cup my hands around the smoke and focus on channeling my energy. I want this to swirl. I want to create a dust devil. With that intention in mind, I feel the tendrils start swirling in the palm of my hand.

Within seconds, the swirling cloud grew bigger and bigger. Once it reaches three feet tall, I take a step back. It looked like a mini-tornado surrounding the incense. I admire my creation. Then, with a quick swat of my hand through the tornado, it disappears into a small stream of smoke like before.

I take a step back and look at The Community, feeling my heart beating fast in my chest as adrenaline runs through my veins.

Everyone is dead silent.

Morgana stepped forward; eyes wider than ever before. "Cur. How the… what?"

"You have all seen what I am capable of," I say in a confident tone. "I can control the four elements of nature."

I gesture to the succulent. "Earth."

To the incense. "Air."

I pick up the water bottle. "Water."

Then I crouch and pick up the candle. "And fire."

I walk toward the crowd. "I will help you all prepare for this battle. Everyone has a gift that can help fight the Dark Shadows. But we all need to keep practicing. I know The Community no longer has a leader to guide and empower us. But I promise to be that leader. But I alone can't win this war or save the world."

I walk over to the far right end of The Community crowd then back the center. "It's up to all of us. Let's win this thing!" I yell, raising my fist up. Everyone starts cheering. Morgana starts shouting out directions for everyone.

Within minutes, everyone began practicing, the sounds of different spells going off causing people to either freeze, be pushed back, or covered in a light-yellow sphere, shielding themselves from the attacks. Suddenly, I see a quick blue spark of electricity in the corner of my eye. Will and Avi are practicing. I know Avi couldn't to the electricity, so it has to be Will.

"Will?" I ask surprised that the bolts electricity came from his hands "I didn't know you could do this!" I exclaim. The two of them stop briefly.

Will looks at me and nods. "Why do you think they call me the tech guy?" he says with a chuckle. "I've had this power for a while now, but I don't use it on people unless I need to. And the perfect test dummy is Avi because he can just bring himself back," he says with a shrug.

I nod and continue walking around, seeing everyone prepare. I am just waiting until the dummy is free so I can use my powers in self-defense.

I walk back to the dummy, seeing Morgana encouraging Leo to continue punching it. I never thought I'd ever see Leo doing anything involving violence, but this is the ultimate picture I won't ever get out of my mind.

"Hey, Cur. Let's see you use your powers against this guy." Leo pats the dummy on the back. I shrug and walk over.

"Everyone get back," I yell as Morgana and Leo move the dummy toward the middle of warehouse. Everyone starts moving toward the sides.

I look at Morgan and Leo, who start taking a few steps back. Morgana nods, giving me the signal to start. I rub my palms together, feeling the warmth of fire. I outstretch my hands and release a large stream of fire, followed by a blast of wind that forced the dummy back a few feet. Then I aim my hands at the floor by the dummy, causing the floor to crack and bounce the dummy back upright.

I think fire, air, and earth are fine for now. I turn around and see Morgana and Leo behind me, wide-eyed. Even the other Community members just froze in their spots. I hate being the center of attention, but at least they know who is probably the most powerful one here. And I don't need to do a lot of practice.

"Alrighty, Cur, let's have you fight against someone," Morgana tells Avi. He walks over to the spot where the dummy was earlier.

"Fight Curanda," she tells him.

"I am going to go easy on you so don't worry," Avi says with his hands at his sides, palms facing upward.

"Bring it on," I say while rubbing my palms together.

Immediately, Avi swings his hand forward as if he had a rope of some form. That's when I feel something tug at my right arm. Oh, no. Avi pulls this invisible rope back, pulling me forward. I don't like this. I place a palm on the floor, commanding the ground to assist me. Suddenly the ground beneath Avi cracks, causing him to stumble then I outreach my left hand, sending him flying back with a gust of wind. His body hits the warehouse wall, sending a loud echo.

Oh, shit.

I get up as soon as Avi's body falls to the ground. Morgana runs past me and crouches beside Avi. Suddenly, his body jerks and he open his eyes. "He's okay," Morgana yells to everyone with a thumbs up.

I look down at the palms of my hands.

I am powerful.

And I will help save us all.

JUNE 11TH, 2019

"Everyone, your final essay is due tomorrow evening at 5 p.m.," Professor Nguyen exclaims as everyone packs up their things, ready to head out. Morgana and I are so stressed out given the fact that tomorrow is the solar eclipse. *The war.* Yeah, this huge-ass impending doom, yet we're here trying to bring some normalcy into our lives by learning about digital media.

We both know that we're so not doing that. Or maybe we should. It'll help us calm down before the eclipse. We begin our trek back to The Community. Max has been gone for the past week and hasn't shown up ever since I left for Joshua Tree. Will went to his apartment room and found the door open, revealing a huge mess of things all over the place. We think he might've moved out or just decided to stay with Harden and his crew.

We've been asking Leo to gather some insight on him, but he still just sees darkness with Max. He can't see where Max is at all. It's just completely black. So, The Community and I have placed another protective spell to ensure that Max does not enter. With all our collective power in the spell, we figured Max wouldn't have access to the building. We also had Will change the keypad in case. We cannot have Max come back for safety reasons.

I feel that if he were to come back that he'd try to manipulate me into joining him. I'd rather not take that risk, considering what I am capable of. Although I could just burn him. But I cannot ever garner the strength to kill him. I have this feeling deep down that there's still a bit of light in him. That maybe the Max I fell for is still there. I just remember Quetzal's advice to help with memory. I just wonder when I will be able to use that advice.

"So, will you ever try peyote?" Morgana asks while we wait at the stoplight. At lease I have the best friend ever to ground me in reality.

I shake my head. "Not in a million years. But then again, maybe I'd transcend into the heavens given my powers."

"I never thought of that," she says while walking. "Do you think anyone who's like us ever took psychedelics?"

"I am sure Avi has," I say, remembering his tie-dyed shirts.

"Yeah, he probably has. From what I heard, he's tried every drug and was able to come back."

"Oh, yeah, he's able to do that. He told me whenever he goes to raves, he takes like lethal doses of Molly, acid, and booze, but he's able to come back like nothing."

"Damn. Must be nice." Morgana is out of breath from trekking up the hill toward our place. We're about half a block away. Suddenly, I hear a familiar voice behind me.

"Curanda,"

I turn around slowly. *It's Max.*

"Shit," Morgana says under her breath.

"Max. How lovely for you to turn up again," I say sarcastically, crossing my arms over my chest. "Heard you left like the filthy cheater you are."

"Ah, he very much is a cheater." A girl with light purple hair walks up from behind him, wearing all black.

"Violet?" asks Morgana.

Violet ignores her. "Max here is also a very, very excellent lover." She walks over to him, puts her hands on the sides of face, and plants a long-ass kiss.

I feel a stabbing pain deep down. I feel like crying, like destroying everything. Hell, if I could, I'd burn Violet to ashes.

"You bitch," I say, clenching my fists at my side. My rage is insanely powerful right now. I am doing everything I can to not show my true powers. It would be a death sentence if I do.

"What do you want?" Morgana asks since I am too clouded in rage. Morgana steps in front of me, protecting me.

"We just came to visit the good ole Community," she says while leaning against Max, who is very happily holding her.

"Sure, you did," I reply. "Max isn't welcomed at The Community anymore."

"And why is that?" He's now speaking. I look at him, anger filling me with rage.

"You abandoned us. You've been a total ass to everyone. We know this isn't the real you, Max," I reply.

"That's preposterous. I am Max Gray and have always been me. I didn't change." He looks down at Violet. "I just found my true calling and my true love."

"Love!" I exclaim as I push Morgana aside and step forward, getting as close as possible to Max. "You cheated on me for this bitch? After all we had been though, after all those romantic nights, all those happy memories of us, and yet you love *her*."

"Maybe *this* bitch has something you lack," Violet responds with a grin. She takes a step away from Max, for good reason.

I am ready to kill them both. But I hold back my powers. I quickly run toward Violet and slap her so hard, leaving a red mark on her pale skin. Violet steps back, cupping her face.

Oh, shit. This is getting good.

She turns around, with her arms at her sides, her palms facing upward. Suddenly, her eyes turn completely black and she starts screaming a high-pitched, blood-curdling scream. I cover my ears and nearly trip walking backward as black orbs begin to grow in her palms.

Oh, shit.

"Run!" Morgana yells. We turn and run as fast as we can, hoping to make it back to The Community. I feel the heat of one her orbs as it zooms by me, missing me by mere inches. With adrenaline in my veins, my feet pound against the pavement.

God damnit! We need safety.

We finally get to the door, input the code, and run inside, locking it behind us. We hear a thud against the door.

"What's going on?" Will says just as he was about to leave, carrying his backpack.

"Max," I say while out of breath. "He's here."

"And I think he has a banshee. With that scream, it's definitely one," says Morgana.

"Shit," Will says while we look back at the door, hearing another thud. "That door can't hold for long." Will places his palms outward, allowing the blue tendrils of electricity to form a protective barrier around the entrance.

"Yeah. Tell everyone to stay inside. Max is here. Be careful," Morgana calls Leo to warn everyone else.

"How do we get rid of them?" Morgana asks. I look at Will, hoping for answers.

"I don't know," he replies. That's not something I'd like to hear from Will. He usually knows everything.

"What's a protective charm we can use? Anything?" I ask, desperate for answers.

Suddenly, the door bursts into pieces. Chunks fly everywhere. Morgana, Will, and I get up from where we were knocked, ready to defend.

We look at Max, Violet, and another person I absolutely hate.

Madison.

Even though my hands are shaking, I am prepared to fight to the death.

"Ah, Curanda." Madison takes a step forward. "So happy to see you again," she says in the most annoying sweet voice.

"Fuck off," I reply, clenching my fists at my sides.

"Aren't you sad that your boyfriend left you for someone who's immensely prettier?" she mocks me, throwing that metaphorical punch to that sensitive part of me. But I am not backing down.

"Not really. Seems like banshee-ass Violet loves Max. Go figure," I say with a shrug.

Madison laughs, putting her hands in her pockets. "Oh, Curanda. So weak and childish."

"What do you want?" I ask.

"Isn't it obvious? We just need you to come with us. If you do so willingly, nobody will die," she says while gesturing to Will and Morgana behind me.

"And if I don't?"

Madison laughs, her bright red eyes meeting my gaze, sending chills down my spine. "We'll kill the whole Community. And not just you guys. But your families and friends."

"No," Morgana says behind me.

"She's bluffing," I console Morgana as I step forward, taking up the challenge.

"Oh, I am certainly not kidding, Cur. So, you better just give yourself to us freely and nobody gets hurt."

"Fuck you," I say while channeling my energy to my palms.

Suddenly, Will and Morgana scream as they are thrown back against the wall, knocked unconscious. I swing my arm in front, propelling Madison and everyone back toward the street. I run outside away from The Community. I can't risk Madison raiding the apartment. I run as fast I can, hoping to lose them down these still confusing side streets.

I hear them running behind me, just a few feet away. *Dammit.*

I keep running, feeling the adrenaline in my veins. I have to keep going. I must protect The Community. I turn around and see Violet transforming into a wolf-like creature. It's horrifying, all black with bright eyes. Its skeletal head has patches of rotten flesh, its jaw filled with sharp teeth dripping blood. It lets out blood-curdling howl.

I run faster, hoping to find shelter behind a car or something. That's when I notice a Jeep. I run toward it, climb the side ladder, and step on the roof. The wolf circles the car, hitting it to knock me over, I hold on as best as I could, and I channel my powers in my hands.

Fire, I need you.

Right as the hound tries to strike, I unleash a burst of fire, burning it. I hear its squeals of pain echo in the distance, but I keep burning it, hoping it will die. I let a few moments go by and stop. The thing is now just pure ashes.

Thank God.

I look around, not seeing Max or Madison anywhere.

They must've—

Wait.

NO.

I realize that The Community is left open, weak and vulnerable.

I run back as fast I can, hoping Madison and Max just left. I knew deep down they did something. I get closer and I see the front door covered in ash and smoke. I walk through the entrance, making sure they aren't in sight. I open the staircase door and headed down the stairs, toward B-floor, seeing the keypad destroyed. The door is still closed. I open it slowly.

Max and Madison have everyone tied up in the center of the Training Room, all three doors hanging off the hinges, the smell of smoke filling my nostrils. I glance at the library and see black flames engulfing it, the same flames in the other rooms.

They destroyed everything.

"Poor Curanda is so weak." Madison says as she moves her hand back in a quick motion. She's holding a knife. "She doesn't care about any of you." She looks toward Max. "Bring Morgana."

Max pushes Morgana down on her knees, her hands tied behind her back, duct tape against her lips. Her screams are muffled by the tape.

"She says she cares so much about The Community, being all brave and all, and look..." She couches down, pointing the tip of the knife at Morgana. "But when everyone is in danger, she takes off. Running away like the pathetic creature she is. Max, hold her. I want to make this one slow and steady."

Max holds Morgana in place, making sure her throat is exposed.

"It's too bad Curanda let you die."

I channel my energy to the knife, wanting it away from them. Within milliseconds, the knife is knocked out of her hands.

"What the—?"

I kick open the door, holding my palms out with orange orbs in them. "You want me so damn bad, take me then. Leave them alone."

"Ha, Curanda. So weak," Madison says. Suddenly, a knife comes flying at me. I block it with a ball of fire from my hands, burning the knife to a pulp. I try to channel my energy at her in retaliation but it's too late. I feel an invisible force hold me in place. I fight the hold, trying to channel my energy to break free but it's too strong.

"See. All you had to do was let us take you. That's it."

"Let the others go," I say while frozen in place.

Madison chuckles then turns to Max. "Kill them all."

I struggle against the invisible grip. I meet Max's eyes. "Don't," I whisper under my breath. A tear streams down my cheek.

Max glances quickly at me then to The Community members, bound and vulnerable.

"*Noxium,*" Max says while snapping his fingers. Everyone collapses.

"No," I scream, wanting to fall to my knees but stuck in this horrendous frozen state, tears streaming down my cheek as I feel a pain deep within my core.

I failed everyone.

Madison walks up to me, smiling. "I won't do the honors of knocking you out. I'll let your lovely ex do it."

I close my eyes, bracing for the pain.

But there was no pain.

Just darkness.

CHAPTER 10

JUNE 12TH, 2019

THE COMMUNITY, MIDNIGHT

"Yeah. I messaged everyone to stay on campus for our safety. This is just..."

Morgana starts to hear voices.

"This is bad. So bad. We're screwed for this war. How are we going to manage the bodies? Avi must be dead if he hasn't come back by now? You can't do anything with your clairvoyant powers?"

"Unfortunately, not."

It's Leo. He's talking to someone else. Morgana needs to see who. She opens her eyes slowly, blinking them back to focus.

It's Zack, from the fifth floor. Morgana starts moving, struggling against the bindings, and tries calling to them.

Finally, Leo hears her and runs over. "Morgana! This is going to hurt," he says while peeling off a corner of the duct tape. With a quick motion, he yanks the tape off.

"Shit!" Morgana yells while catching her breath.

"What happened?" Leo asks.

"They… raided the place."

"Who's they?"

"Max and Madison came here. They took Curanda,"

"What?" exclaims Leo as he looks at everyone else. Within seconds, more eyes start opening.

"They're alive," says Morgana, quickly looking around then meeting Leo's gaze. "Can you salvage a knife from the Apothecary?"

Leo looks up toward the burnt doorway. "I'll see what I can find." He runs across the room toward the Apothecary. Everything has been charred to ashes. Broken glass litters the floor, a few melted multicolored candles drip from the broken shelves. The wooden cabinets that held the tools are completely destroyed.

"There's no way we can find a knife here," Leo says while examining the room, seeing the shards of broken glass by his feet. "This might work, but—"

"Hey, I see something on the floor," Zack exclaims.

"Where?"

"It's underneath the sink."

Leo takes out his phone and flashes the light on it. It's a knife, perfectly intact. Somehow, it withstood the black flames. Leo grabs the knife and heads back to everyone and removes the rope bindings. It's going to take a while considering how thick the rope is and there's about ten Community members.

Leo and Zack alternate cutting the cords on everyone's hands and feet then let everyone else remove the duct tape.

"Wait," Leo says as he approaches Sabrina. He turns her over, seeing a pile of dried blood staining the carpet. "Sabrina?" Leo asks while inspecting her. He places the knife down and reaches for her wrist in hopes of feeling a heartbeat.

There's none.

"We need help!" Leo yells while removing her cords.

"What's going on?" exclaims Zack as he walks over to Leo. "Dammit," he says under his breath.

"Is everyone okay?" Morgana asks as everyone begins to remove the duct tape.

"We lost Sabrina," says Leo as he gazes at Morgana.

"Shit." She shakes her head. Although she used to hate Sabrina, the pain of her loss still affects her. "Wait, is Avi awake?"

Leo and Zack look for Avi.

"Avi!" yells Zack as he walks over to his body lay and starts shaking him, hoping he'll be alive.

"What?!" Avi wakes up, startled. "What happened?"

"No time to explain. Get up. Sabrina is dead."

"Oh, shit." Avi gets up and joins the crowd of people starting to surround her.

"Is there any way to bring her back?" Morgana asks as she joins Leo, who's crouched over Sabrina.

Avi kneels beside her. "I might be able to, but it looks like she's been dead for hours." He turns her over, revealing the dried bloodstain on the floor. "I'll see what I can do."

"Let's hope she'll come back," says Morgana as she eyes everyone else. "I can't believe this." She stands up, shaking from the shock.

"What do we do now?" Akasha asks.

Morgana looks at the broken door where Madison and Max broke in.

"We fight."

THE DARK SHADOWS 3 A.M.

Pain. That's all I can feel right now. It's all over my body. I can't bear it any longer. I just want relief. It's draining me so much. I don't even feel human anymore. A deep voice breaks the silence, temporarily distracting me from the pain.

"She's… key to all this."

Me? I am a key to... what?

All of this confuses me. The last thing I remember was seeing Morgana almost killed and then... everything is fuzzy after that. I've just been in darkness for God knows how long. Then the pain started. It feels like I've been dealing with this forever.

"Is the child awake?" A hoarse voice breaks the darkness.

"Yes, my lord," says an all-too-familiar voice. I slowly blink my eyes open, the temporary blurriness revealing a scene I never thought I'd see.

Madison is kneeling in front of… a goat.

No. It's a gigantic goat-like creature, about the size of a person covered in a long robe with a red inverted pentagram etched into the fabric.

"Ah. Yes." The creature rises from the throne. Its horrendous horns pierce out of its skull, its hooves echoing in this cave. I am starting to realize how hot it is as I feel a drop of sweat stream down my forehead.

I try moving my hands free but utter pain spreads throughout my body. Metal cuffs dig into my wrists as I try pulling free. Whenever I move, the jaggedness of the stone pierces my neck and back.

Where the hell am I?

The goat creature approaches, tall, ugly, and just evil. It stretches out its grotesque hand, stroking my cheek. I close my eyes, trying to look away. "We've been waiting so long for you, child."

I stay silent. This thing terrifies me.

"We have, my lord." Madison rises and walks over toward the goat creature. "Curanda has immense potential for the second coming."

"What… second coming?" I can barely get the words out without feeling the stabbing pain in my back.

"Oh, child." The goat creature gets closer. I can smell the mixture of its stench and sulfur. "You have no idea what's happening." He turns around and walks toward the right side of the cave. "My army will finally rise and take over this wretched planet." He gazes upward, toward the ceiling of the cave.

"Those Light Beings above left this planet for humanity to roam free. Of course, they gave a small number of those humans gifts. But, of course, there're rules." He stomps his foot. "Damn rules." He gazes at Madison. "They do nothing but hold us back. Prevent us from being the all-powerful beings we are meant to be."

"I don't understand," I say.

"Of course, you wouldn't," the creature responds. "You see, with the powers we have, we were considered Gods. GODS, I TELL YOU," he shouts with his arms outstretched, revealing long claws.

"But no. The Light Beings above wouldn't have that. So, they called the powers 'gifts.'" He walks back toward me. "Just so happens the Light Beings decided that you would be bestowed with the most powerful one of all." He approaches closer again. I am so grossed out seeing the drool drip from his snout. I turn away, avoiding this sickening scene.

"You see, Child of Light, I need that power you possess so that I can set my army free."

"For what?" I ask, averting my gaze. Suddenly, a strong force out of my control moves my face back to his, my eyes open, focusing on the goat creature.

"This planet needs cleansing. It needs renewal. There's too much chaos. And my army and I can fix that." He turns to Madison. "By creating an apocalypse."

Apocalypse?

"Also known as The Second Coming," says Madison as she gazes at me. I keep breathing heavily, trying to breath in air. But of course, all I keep breathing in is musty air.

"So, you guys need me to start this apocalypse?"

"Exactly," says the goat creature. "We will wipe this planet clean. And rebuild from a clean slate." He steps back and looks at the ceiling. "In this world, we'll be considered Gods as we should've been."

Me? A goddess? No way.

"Child," he says, while looking at me, "You can reign as queen of this new world. Capable of whatever you please." He walks over to me again. "You can rule beside me." His long nail strokes my cheek. "We can be the most powerful beings in the universe."

"Wait, Lucius." Madison's voice makes him turn around. "You promised I would be the most powerful witch alive! You told me I'd rule as queen, not her."

"Oh, Madison. How naive you are."

"Wha—" As soon as she says this, she goes flying against the cave wall. Chains protrude from the ceiling and clamp down on her arms and feet. The chains lift her and push her against the wall.

Lucius walks over to her. "You were never important. I just used your mortal body to allow me to fulfill my desires of death and destruction. It's because of you I found Curanda." He stretches out his hand. Suddenly Madison is gagging. He's choking her.

"You pathetic excuse of a witch. The only thing you gave me was the child. And a good killing spree. That was truly enjoyable." He squeezes his hand in a fist. Suddenly, Madison goes silent with one last gag. Her head drops to her chest in defeat.

Holy shit.

"Thank hell that annoying witch is dead." He looks back to me. "We have so much work to do."

"Work?"

"Oh, yes, child." He stares up at the ceiling. "It's only a matter of time before the eclipse will occur. But I need someone to make you weak so that you will not resist."

"Make me weak? I will never be weak."

"We'll see about that." He turns around to his throne. "Slave. Come forth."

I look toward the throne.

No. NO.

Max comes out from behind the throne. "Yes, my Lord."

"Keep Curanda busy. Make sure she's as weak as possible. I'd rather not have to put up a fight. I have matters to attend to in the meantime." He walks away toward the back of the cave, disappearing.

Max walks toward me with a stupid grin I've learned to hate.

"Ah, Curanda. So good to see you again." He walks up to me, getting so close. "Sleep well?"

"Fuck off," I tell him while feeling the pain of the rock inch deeper in my back. "How could you?"

"How could I what?" he replies sarcastically.

I shake my head, a tear streaming down my face. "You killed The Community. You, the most loyal leader who cared so much for us, uniting us all, have gone completely rogue."

"I didn't go rogue, Cur." His gray eyes meet mine. "I found out what I am truly destined for."

"Which is being a slave for some evil goat creature?" I ask, laughing. "That's some life you found."

He chuckles. "I can't wait to be known as a God. I mean, who wouldn't want that?"

"When the whole world is enslaved by the Dark Shadows? How could you want to rule that? Rule death and destruction?"

He shrugs. "I'll come to enjoy it when The Second Coming happens."

I shake my head, looking down at the floor. "I remember the first time you told me about The Dark Shadows." That's when I hear Quetzalcoatl's voice in the back of my mind: *Ground him with memory.*

"You saw me reading the necromancer book when I first trained with Avi. You told me Giger's work is one every necromancer must have, yet you weren't a necromancer yourself."

"That's the old m—"

"We used to meet at your apartment on the first floor a few times a week. I asked you everything about Wicca, asked you how I could be a better at spell casting. I remember when we went on our first date." I look out in the distance.

"We ended up walking to the botanical gardens and claimed our spot in the garden. You even convinced the people there to leave so we could have it all to ourselves. We carved our initials in the bamboo stalks."

A tear streams down my cheek.

"Then you kissed me. It was the first genuine kiss that I ever felt." Another tear streams down. "A few months down the road, that spot was the place you said 'I love you' for the first time." Now I am full on crying, wanting to stop because of the pain. But I keep on talking. "When I first moved in your place, those sweet mornings.. You told me you'd love me no matter what happens."

Max looks down at the floor with an emotionless expression.

"You've changed so much. This isn't you, Max." I close my eyes, wishing for the pain to end, wishing for all of this to end.

Suddenly, I feel something against my face. I don't flinch. At this point, it doesn't matter what happens to me.

"Cur." I open my eyes, seeing Max inches from my face. His hands cup my face. I close my eyes, not wanting to know what pain will come next. Suddenly, I feel his lips on mine.

What the—?

I open my eyes, gazing into his eyes.

"I'm free."

"What? I don't understand."

He smiles. I feel the warmth radiating off him. "I don't hear that horrible voice in the back of my head. It used to control me. Used to tell me horrible things that would happen had I not listened to it."

"Wait," I say, while realization dawns on me. "Were you in control this entire time?"

"Not really. I felt trapped. There was this other voice that would control me. I couldn't feel my body. Couldn't stop what I was doing. I was able to see what I was doing but incapable of doing anything about it."

He looks down at the floor then meets my gaze.

"I'm so sorry about what I did to you. That's what hurts me the absolute most. I'd never do that to you and seeing what that other voice made me do almost completely broke me."

"It wasn't the real you who did that all of that. I'm just happy you're back to your true self. I know you'd never do all of those things."

"I'm glad to be back too. And I promise to make things right again."

I smile and nod when the realization of The Community hit me.

"Wait. So, you saw what was happening to The Community?"

He nods. "It pained me so much seeing it all. Thank God you showed up right on time before Madison took out any more people."

"Wait. Did she kill anyone?"

"She did stab Sabrina but I'm not sure who else."

"Oh, shit," I say while glancing at the floor then meeting his gaze. I need to ask the question I dread the most. "Did you kill The Community?"

"Are you kidding?!" he exclaims. "I would never let anything happen to them. I managed to fight the voice off for just a moment. I just made everyone pass out. Madison was too dumb to see it," he says with a grin. "Okay, now I have to see how to free you," he says while looking around.

"Can you use magic?" I ask.

"I don't think so. But even if I do, I don't know how to escape." He looks at the other side of the cave then back at me, lost.

"I think we're just going to have to blend in," I say. "Pretend you're under that spell or whatever it was. That way, Lucius won't get suspicious."

"Good point," he replies

2 p.m.

"UCLA's astronomy team is set up outside the Math Sciences building for the viewing of the Solar Eclipse happening in about an hour. It is anticipated…" Morgana shuts off the TV in the common area. This place used to have Max at the podium talking about The Council's rules. Now it's Morgana leading the meeting.

"Everyone," she shouts to the forty or so people in the room. "We need to wake the fuck up now! We have to fight. We need to save Cur. We can't have her power in the wrong hands." Morgana swallows back tears. "Let's give this war all that we got!" She raises her fist in the air.

The Community turns into a roar of shouts. "Alrighty. Everyone gear up with whatever you have in your apartments. Someone check on Avi's progress too," Morgana says as she heads upstairs. She opens her closet, revealing her wooden trunk with a large pentagram etched across it. She opens it and scans all the wands, books, herbs, and oils then finds her large two nine-inch-long metal athames tucked into their leather holders.

"So sorry, God and Goddess. But I need to use these." She puts them on the seam of her pants and rises from the floor. "We got a war to fight." She runs out of her apartment to staircase, hearing footsteps from the people coming down it from the other floors. As Morgana reaches the bottom, she meets Leo's gaze.

"You don't have a weapon besides the amulet?"

He shakes his head. "Ian and I only have one sharp knife in our apartment and no one else has an extra."

"Hang on." She reaches for one of the athames and hands it to him.

His eyes widen, seeing the length of it. "How do I uh…?"

"You'll be fine. Just trust your intuition and your survival mode will kick in."

"Okay," he replies and takes a few breaths

"Let's do this." Morgana pats him on the back and walks over to the crowd of Community members who create a path for Morgana lead in front. Avi, Will, and Leo follow suit, standing directly behind her with their weapons. She steps out onto the sidewalk, scanning the area.

Not a soul in sight. Suddenly, the sky begins to darken, turning into a mix of day and night. Morgana's breathing quickens, her body feeling tense as she steps onto the street, waiting for what's to come. She starts to recite defense spells in her mind to remember when the danger happens, but her nerves are making the words jumbled.

Suddenly, the ground begins to shake.

Morgana hears the screams of a few Community members as she loses her balance, falling to the ground below, her athame falling a few feet away. She crawls toward it to grasp the handle. Suddenly, the asphalt starts to crack, revealing a bright orange glow underneath, her athame lying on the other side. She gets the handle and while pulling it away, something grabs her arm.

A deformed hand pulls her arm down as she holds on to the athame for dear life. Finally, with as much strength that she can muster, she frees her arm and unsheathes her athame. She crawls back and looks around, seeing more cracks start to form with and hands beginning to rise all the way down the street. Morgana stares, wide-eyed.

As Morgana returns her gaze forward, the hand grips the edge, climbing up onto the pavement revealing a hideous zombie-like creature. It stands upright, its eyes bright red orbs that reveal its humanoid skull. It smiles, revealing hundreds of sharp fangs.

It screeches and lunges at Morgana. Without time to use her spells, she reaches for athame and slices the creature, hoping to wound it. Then Avi comes out of nowhere and slices it with a sword.

"Can't we use magic?" she yells to him.

"No. They won't budge with the most powerful defensive spell. Tried it."

"Dammit," Morgana says as she realizes this athame will only help her for so long.

This needs to end.

DARK SHADOWS—2 P.M.
"The Eclipse is upon us," Lucius says as he gets closer to me once more. I glance at Max, who's trying his hardest to remain menacing-looking. Lucius grabs my chin with his hand, making me look him in his goat eyes.

"It's time, child." He takes a step back, stretches his hands out in front of me and begins chanting incoherent words.

Suddenly, I feel excruciating pain. It's as if the life is being sucked out of me, deep pain felt to the bone. I scream in agony, wanting it to stop. I try channeling my energy to stop it.

"You can't stop me, child. I will gladly enjoy absorbing your powers," he says with a menacing laugh.

I try fighting against him. I need to stay strong.

But my vision darkens once more.

3 p.m.

Intense heat warms my body. The smell of dirt fills my nostrils, making me slowly open my eyes.

I am back in Joshua Tree at the very spot I met Quetzalcoatl.

"Curanda," Quetzalcoatl calls. I blink a few times and finally see him, covered in green armor.

"What's happening?" I ask.

"You must stay strong." He walks over to where I am sitting. "You are capable of controlling all of the five elements in the universe. Your name is that of the most powerful Curandera alive. You can defeat the darkness."

"How?" I ask, desperate for answers.

"Use the fifth element."

He stretches out his hand, revealing a bright white orb of light. It feels so familiar, comforting and powerful. I reach for it, cupping it in my hands.

Spirit.

The white orb glows brighter and bigger.

Once it us the size of a basketball, I push the orb of light within in.

I feel the pain ease, I feel… weightless. Everything glows white.

I am Spirit, Earth, Fire, Water, and Air.

I am...

Pentalpha.

DARK SHADOWS

Lucius smiles and laughs. "It's nearly complete." Curanda's body hangs lifeless from the chains, her head bend down as her power is begins to drain from her body. Max can't let this continue. He has to fight.

Suddenly, Curanda slowly raises her head. Her eyes are no longer brown. They are white orbs of light. Her whole body begins to glow.

"What in…?" As Lucius takes a step back away from Curanda, Max shouts.

"*Rediro!*" Lucius goes flying toward the other side of the cave. He didn't think the spell would work here.

But it does.

Right as Lucius rises from the floor, ready to destroy Max, the sound of metal breaking fills the cave. As Curanda's body begins to rise, the chains break loose from their hold on her. The ceiling of the cave begins to crack as she ascends, allowing light to flow through. Curanda continues to rise with her hands stretched high, carrying white light in her palms. The ground appears farther and farther from her. Until she reaches the white clouds above.

She's transcending.

CURANDA

I am able to see the ground faintly through the veil of light covering my eyes. The world is getting smaller as I feel weightless. I look upward and reach my palms out. I know the words I need to say to end this war once and for all.

"By the power of light, let there be peace upon this world. Let not evil control this planet. By the power of light and love, I command evil to die." And with these words, I let the orbs of light emanate from my palms. I am covered in white light.

Suddenly, the sky is covered in white light. As if an explosion occurred, an explosion of peace. Of light. Of love.

THE COMMUNITY

"I can't hold them off any longer!" Avi yells while swinging his sword, cutting another zombie creature in half.

Morgana is exhausted. Her athame can only take one more hit before it'll start to damage. There are still too many of them. But she still has to fight. One of the creatures lunges at her and she stabs it a few times and runs back, her blade snapped in half.

She hears another creature screech behind her, another two flank her sides. She's completely surrounded.

She's going to die.

"Avi!" she screams right as one of the creatures lunges at her. She prepares for the pain, the agony that is yet to come. She closes her eyes, hoping to not see the last moments of her life. Tears stream down her face.

But there is no pain.

She opens her eyes. Bright white light breaks through the darkness. The zombie creatures surrounding her melt onto the ground and the cracks begin to seal, returning to street to solid asphalt. The sun begins to shine, and The Community members look around in wonder. All of them made it out of this alive. Morgana looks down at her athame, expecting the blade to be bent in half.

But it's not. It's as if it was completely brand new.

"What the hell?" Morgana says while picking it up, turning it around to ensure that it's real.

"Hey, everyone!" Avi yells in the distance.

She turns around, seeing Avi farther down the street. She follows the other Community members toward Avi, wondering why he called them over. As she approaches, there's a crowd of more Community members surrounding two people, one of whom has the recognizable blond hair.

No way.

CURANDA

I begin to slowly descend, feeling the white light still glowing off my skin. I descend lower, and my vision clears. I can see the world below slowly coming into focus as I near closer to the cave to save Max. The opening of the cave widens as I descend closer, finally feeling my feet on the ground, waiting for the battle with the Dark Shadow Lord.

I look around. And see no one. Not even Max.

"Max?" I yell while feeling my nerves kick into gear, fearing that the worst has happened to him. Suddenly, I hear a voice coming from the back of the cave.

"Cur?" I run toward the back.

It's him.

I walk closer, scanning him from head to toe, making sure he's okay.

"Did… did anything happen? Are you hurt?" I start asking a lot of questions as adrenaline courses through my veins.

"It's okay, Cur, I'm fine."

"But what about that demon lord?"

"Well, I managed to wound him but you destroyed him."

"I did?"

He nods. "When you started ascending, there was so much white light that came into the cave that it burned him to ashes."

"Holy shit," I exclaim. "That is so cool. I can't believe I did that."

"I can't believe it either."

I smile and lean in closer. He wraps his arms around me as I meet his gaze, entranced by those beautiful gray eyes I love. "I'm so happy it's over."

"Me too."

June 18th, 2019, 2 p.m.
I can't believe we survived the war, aced finals, and managed to get The Community back on track all within a matter of days. I'm still in awe about how powerful I am considering that I mastered every element known to man and destroyed the darkness that sought to take over the world. That's something to be proud of.

I thought I'd reward myself with a peaceful visit to The Botanical Gardens, to my favorite spot where Max and I kissed for the very first time. I follow the winding path that leads to the spot hidden by the bamboo trees that circle around it.

I place my purse on the stone bench and sit, admiring all the greenery of the leaves from the bushes. I turn around and find the bamboo stalk, seeing our initials carved into it.

Suddenly, I hear rustling coming from the bushes in the side. It's not really a path but people sometimes step there anyway. I look toward the sounds and smile. "Max?"

He reaches for the bamboo for balance and nearly trips trying to get to our spot.

"Even after having won the most epic war in history, you're still a goofball."

He laughs. "Can't help it. It's in my DNA."

We both laugh. He walks over to me, and we embrace.

"You saved the world, Cur."

I shake my head. "We all did."

He smiles.

And so do I.

ACKNOWLEDGMENTS

There are so many people I'd like to thank for allowing me to make this dream of mine come true. Thank you so much, Mom and Dad, for supporting me in all that I do and for allowing me to fulfill this long-time dream of mine. You have been there with me for this entire journey and gave me the motivation to continue pursuing this dream even when times were tough. That's the greatest gift you can give me and the greatest lesson that you've taught me. Thank you, Anthony, for being the best brother you can ever be who supported this book nerd in creating a story of her own. I would like to thank the rest of my family for supporting this dream and helping me create my very first novel. I would like to thank my friends from UCLA, Annie, Leon, and Bill.

You have all been with me on both my journey in college and in writing this book. You have all supported me through this and allowed me to show how your friendships have changed my life and to remember all the memories we've made.

I'd like to thank all the people I have met in the New Age community who have inspired the creation of the magic in story. Thank you so much to April Pfender for teaching me the wonderful gift of Reiki energy healing and to Helen Vonderheide for giving me the greatest gift of wisdom, healing through the Akashic Records. It'd like to thank all Wiccans and Neo-Pagans I have met along my spiritual journey and my favorite Wiccan author Scott Cunningham. And a big thank you to the author who brought modern magic into my life and inspired my journey into the New Age, Cate Tiernan.

And a huge thank you to entire team at New Degree Press for making this dream become reality. You all have made me become the best author I can be and inspired me to pursue a career involving creative writing. Overall, I am so thankful for everyone who went joined me on this year-long journey to create a beautiful work of art that I will cherish for so many years to come.

www.ingramcontent.com/pod-product-compliance
Lightning Source LLC
LaVergne TN
LVHW011801060526
838200LV00053B/3645